TIDES OF BLESSING

First published in 2022 by
New Life Publishing, Luton,
Bedfordshire LU3 4DQ

© Russ Fairman and John James McKenna

British Library Cataloguing in Publication Data
A catalogue record for this book is available
from the British Library

ISBN 978 1 912237 37 1

Typesetting by New Life Publishing,
Luton, UK www.goodnewsbooks.co.uk
Printed and bound in Great Britain

TIDES OF BLESSING
A SAILING PILGRIMAGE
AROUND THE UK

by

RUSS FAIRMAN
WITH
JOHN JAMES MCKENNA

ABOUT THE AUTHORS

Russ Fairman is a Catholic Christian and experienced sailor, who lives in Southampton. He has been married to Deirdre for nearly 40 years and they have five children and twelve grandchildren, who affectionately call him 'Admiral'. Russ has been a civil engineer, commercial diver, enterprise IT sales manager and tall ship sailing skipper. Over 30 years ago while collecting Deirdre from a Billy Graham event, he found himself standing at the front giving himself to Jesus. Today Russ is an active member of the church, serving in numerous capacities: on the Charis Charismatic Co-ordinating team for England and Wales, the national board for Worldwide Marriage Encounter, the core team for Harvesters Men's Network UK, lecturer for the iBelong School of Personal Transformation, core team for the ecumenical New Carmel Prophetic Hub Network UK, Healing on the Streets Southampton (HOTS) and the celebrate Charismatic Renewal movement, including chairing Celebrate Southampton and leading the Celebrate Sailing Mission. He also finds time to be on the Committee of Warsash Sailing Club, an RYA Cruising Instructor and Skipper for the youth charity, Rona Sailing Project. Russ has an enthusiasm for encouraging others to follow their dreams and live life to the full, which for him means being in a personal relationship with Jesus. This is Russ' first book.

John James McKenna is a father, husband and former business journalist who now edits content for global organisations. After hearing his friend Russ speak about his adventure at the Harvesters conference for Christian men, John knew that this wonderful tale had to be committed to print so that many more could experience the joy that it inspires. The voice you hear in this book is Russ's, captured and written down by John's hand.

PRAISE FOR TIDES OF BLESSING

DREAMS ARE DOORWAYS INTO ANOTHER LIFE; TRANSFORMING A dream into a lifestyle is within all our grasp, and the pages of this book encourage that idea. This is an inspiring book and fills the reader with hope. From the question 'What if it's true?' to the exciting mini-adventures in each chapter, the book oozes with those two sentiments of hope and adventure in competing measure.

I love the Fairmans' demonstration of faith as they embarked upon this adventure together. My take away from the book? We can all be adventurers, if we take a simple step of faith.
Yinka Oyekan, President of the Baptist Union of Great Britain

I COULDN'T STOP READING THIS BOOK ONCE I STARTED! SUCH JOY IN every chapter – so many tangible descriptions of God's presence on the journey. So many lives touched and changed by His Love. Russ and Deirdre have been a much appreciated Celebrate family looking after the crèche at the Ilfracombe conference for many years. We were so excited when Russ came with his dream for the mission although, I confess, that our initial donation was made on condition that we didn't have to crew! To surround our country with a ring of prayer uniting Celebrate Weekends during the voyage was an amazing vision from God. And for Russ, the completion of the trip was not an end but a beginning - taking him into a deeper relationship with our heavenly Father and stepping out into new ministries.

Thank you also to Deirdre for her supporting role – a true safety net of prayer and provision to Russ's commitment. The Celebrate Mission Scroll hangs in our Dining room – a visible reminder of those wonderful 77 days. Listening to Russ talking about the trip, one phrase really stayed with me. He said that sometimes we need to be intentionally vulnerable for God to show us how close He is to us. Help us, Lord, to hear and trust your calling.

Sue Whitehead, co-founder of Celebrate Conferences

IN MEMORY OF DAN BURGESS
February 1985 - December 2019

This book is dedicated to Dan Burgess, a close family friend who crewed the boat through the most challenging parts of the voyage, and an absolute joy to be with. A young man with a family who I'd known and loved for many years through Celebrate, and our mountain biking exploits in Wales.

Dan had a zeal and enthusiasm for the adventure of life, only surpassed by his humility and willingness to help anybody with anything.

Dan's expectations of himself drove him, but also challenged him. We had the time of our lives on this trip together and our parting hug at Plymouth said more than words could express. I miss you my dear friend, rest in peace.

77 Days
2800 Miles
45 Crew
65 Ports visited
12 Celebrate City Gatherings

CONTENTS

INTRODUCTION

THE OLDER YOU BECOME, THE WORSE YOUR HEARING GETS, apparently. But I think that's only true of the kind of listening that you do with your ears. There's another kind of hearing that can take a lifetime to develop.

Lying awake in bed one night, my wife Deirdre sleeping soundly beside me, I found myself puzzling: what is this so-called God-given 'purpose-driven life' that some Christians talk about, and who are these people who say that God speaks to them and guides them?

It certainly wasn't me. On the outside I was a model Christian man: a husband, a dad and grandad, acting as provider in a highly paid commercial job and tinkering with a few charitable religious activities on the side.

But on the inside I felt like a ball bouncing around in a pinball machine, being pushed every which way with no clarity about where I was headed. Lying there in bed I prayed an irreverent prayer born of my frustration: 'Well, God, what do you want from me? What is this life you've given me all about?'

I may have dared to ask the question, but I was too afraid to listen to the answer. Maybe it was precisely this fear of mine that was the problem: maybe it was my fear of what God might say that was causing my inability to hear Him. All I know is that, lying there, I suspected what God's answer might be, and I knew my response would be: 'That's just way too scary, I can't do that, I can't let go of things that I rely on to define me.' So instead of listening and acting, I yet again found myself choosing to stay right where I was; in an endless loop of trying to discern God's will, while refusing to be changed in any way.

I rolled over and went back to sleep, parking my dreams for another day, or maybe even for another life that I would never live. As John Lennon once sang, 'life is what happens to you while you're busy making other plans'. But something would not let me rest, a kernel of a dream was in me and kept rising up, no matter how much I tried to suppress it.

This story is about what happened when I finally allowed the Lord to untie the ropes that were keeping me moored in a sea of uncertainty. It's about moving in faith rather than certainty. And it is about how, when you start doing this, you really can start to hear God speak.

It may have taken me nearly 60 years to get there, but on this 77-day voyage around the UK, I finally found answers for the questions I asked in my bed in the middle of the night. I finally developed the ability to hear the God I had heard spoken about since a child, the God of school assembly hymns and my old Nan's biblical expressions. Her scriptural turns of phrase were pearls of wisdom baked into everyday dialogue: 'There's none so blind as those who cannot see, forgive and forget, heaven loves a trier.' Every cockney girl born within the sound of Bow Bells from two generations ago knew the Christian story, in sound bites, memorised to keep you on the 'straight and narra'. These seeds were sown by Nanna in me, but they took time to grow: God's time, which can be a lifetime.

My life's journey toward hearing God speak finally found its destination in a prayer mission sailing around Britain. What this 77-day watery pilgrimage covering 2,800 miles and 12 cities taught me is that God holds every single detail of our lives: He has a plan.

But He didn't teach me the easy way. As counter-intuitive as it may sound, my trust in the Lord grew on the mission from those times of difficulty when he left me hanging out there. He would let me reach the point of dismay, and only then intervene - on each occasion stretching my faith further so that the distant God I thought I knew eventually became a personal friend in Jesus.

The Lord also blessed me and those I sailed with, with countless opportunities to pray with strangers, to hug them (do you remember this pre-Covid experience?), and to gather as large groups in public places across the country singing His praises – simple blessings that we perhaps took for granted, but less than a year later would at times be impossible due to the pandemic.

Allow me to take you on this voyage of discovery in this little book, and see where it takes you. My dream is that you will be inspired to dare to dream, to connect with the reality that you are completely loved by God, for who you are and not for what you do, and become the person God created you to be, stepping into the life he has already prepared for you.

Well, come and see: step aboard and join me, 45 crew members, and thousands of others across the UK on this sailing voyage and help crew this little ship into the unknown. You just might be inspired to set off on a journey of your own. One that you've been dreaming of for far too long.

PART ONE

THE EAST COAST

ONE

Plotting an Adventure
(Southampton to Brighton)

'My grace is sufficient for you,
for my power is made perfect in weakness.'
(2 Corinthians chapter 12, verse 9)

OVER THE COURSE OF 24 HOURS FROM FRIDAY 26 TO SATURDAY 27 April 2019, Storm Hannah battered much of the UK. Winds reaching speeds of more than 80 miles per hour moved across the Irish Sea to hit England and Wales, leaving thousands of homes without electricity.

These winds also threatened to end my sailing mission before it had even begun. I was planning to leave Hamble quay near Southampton on Saturday 27th April to begin a three-month voyage around the UK.

It was a trip that was nearly three decades in the making, and which I had been planning in detail for the previous two years. I hoped to not only sail around the UK, but also up many of its great tidal rivers into the hearts of its cities.

I had planned gatherings with Christians from many of these towns, and I had a detailed schedule for picking up and dropping off crewmates along the way.

But all of that planning hung by a thread on that wet and windy Saturday in April. Thirty or so well-wishers – family and friends, Christians from the local area, Sarah Bassett from the local BBC radio station, and several locals who just happened along the quay at the time, including one old lady with a dog who had asked for prayer for her loneliness and was visibly over-whelmed by the welcome she received – braved the weather and gathered at the quayside in Hamble to give me and my crew of three a great send-off.

While it was a wonderful afternoon of celebration with music and much laughter, there would be no boat setting sail as the climax of the event. Storm Hannah had put paid to that.

Not for the last time on this trip, I found myself asking God 'Why Lord? Why have you brought me this far only to leave me hanging? '

As I said, this was a trip that was nearly 30 years in the making. In the early 1990s two enduring passions of my life began, without which this wonderful adventure would have never taken place: I started sailing offshore, and I began taking my then-young family to Devon for the Celebrate Christian family conference. Celebrate began life as a week-long Catholic charismatic event in Ilfracombe at Easter, and has since grown to encompass regional Celebrate weekends that take place up and down the UK throughout the year.

Celebrate was a real blessing to my family over the 15 years that we attended the week-long event in Ilfracombe. The beauty of that week was that the children were developing friendships and discussing their faith in a way that never happened back in our parish church.

However, building similar relationships is much more difficult to do when you just have a weekend, so I wanted to do something to remind everyone that Celebrate is a UK-wide movement and much bigger than the weekend they attend in Southampton, St. Albans, Cardiff or Glasgow.

I also wanted to do something to help offer prayer and healing to a divided country. The 2016 referendum on the UK's membership of the EU had split the country down the middle. I hated the divisive language around Brexit that made everyone either a 'leaver ' or 'remainer '. Those divisions were deep and raw, and the country was hurting. In response, I wanted to put a ring of prayer around the country, to really love it. When someone's stressed or in pain, you can say the right things and offer help. But what really works is just a massive great hug, and I wanted to place a great big prayer hug around the UK.

What led me to believe it could be a sailing mission that might bring together both the Celebrate family across the UK and offer prayer to our divided country - while also inspiring others to follow their God-given dream - was my experience volunteering with the Rona Sailing Project.

This fantastic charity runs therapeutic voyages with various groups: vulnerable teenagers; those undertaking drug and alcohol rehabilitation; and young adults. I have felt great joy witnessing how the environment of a boat can bring together people from all sorts of backgrounds, facing all kinds of challenges, and lead them to take responsibility for themselves and each other, and interact in a positive way. It has led me to view sailing as much more than just a hobby: it is something that can lead to adventures that transform lives forever.

And so the idea of a Celebrate Sailing Mission began to form in my mind. But so did all kinds of doubts: chief among these was that this could be dangerous. If I were to offer crew places to anybody who wanted to be part of this watery pilgrimage, I would be taking complete novices and strangers on the boat and out into the open seas. There was huge potential for disaster, for somebody to go overboard. This mission could end up being a black mark on Celebrate's name. Celebrate could have been criticised for running such an activity or sponsoring it.

The only way to overcome these doubts was to ask the Celebrate leadership if they could support the sailing mission.

I finally summoned up the courage to make this request while sitting in a café one summer's afternoon in Rome. I was there as one of more than 50,000 Catholics who had gathered with Pope Francis in the ancient Circus Maximus during the feast of Pentecost in June 2017. He had invited us there to celebrate the 50th anniversary of the Charismatic Renewal movement in the Catholic Church. The movement began in the United States in

1967, when a group of Catholic students from Duquesne University in Pennsylvania were transformed during a retreat weekend. Their powerful experience of the Holy Spirit on that weekend unleashed a new movement in the Church, with 100 million Catholics today identifying as charismatics.

As charismatics we believe that the outpouring of the Holy Spirit that took place at the first Pentecost 2,000 years ago wasn't a one-off event. We believe the Holy Spirit is alive and active today, continuing to pour out the charismatic gifts identified by St. Paul in his first letter to the Corinthians:

> To each is given the manifestation of the Spirit for the common good. To one is given through the Spirit the utterance of wisdom, and to another the utterance of knowledge according to the same Spirit, to another faith by the same Spirit, to another gifts of healing by the one Spirit, to another the working of miracles, to another prophecy, to another the discernment of spirits, to another various kinds of tongues, to another the interpretation of tongues. *1 Corinthians 12:7-10*

Experiencing the gifts of the Holy Spirit in my own life has taught me that I don't have to try to do everything in my own strength - even though, being a stubborn man, I usually try to. As a result, it has also been a recurring lesson for me over the past 30 years since I began attending Celebrate with my family. And it was one that the Lord would start shouting loudly at me during the sailing mission.

Over that time of both attending Celebrate week conference and serving as part of my local weekend Celebrate team, I have built up great friendships with fellow celebrators across the country. It capped off a great day of celebrations in Circus Maximus – the former chariot-racing arena turned into an open-air praise party - to be walking through the streets of Rome with my wife, Deirdre, and to bump into our dear friends Jenny and Paul Baker.

After greeting each other with the thoroughly un-British hugs and kisses, we walked together to a nearby café. Jenny at that time was regional co-ordinator for all of the Celebrate weekends that take place across the UK. Huddled together in that tiny café I knew that this was the moment to test whether the idea of the mission was more than just one of Russ' hare-brained schemes. It was time to see if this really was something that God was in, and something that Celebrate could support.

My mouth was drying and my palms sweaty as I said: 'Jenny I've got something I would like to talk to you about. '

I laid out the whole idea. It was like a prospectus for the trip: what it was, how it could be a common activity for all the weekends across the UK to be involved in, and how it could take prayer around the country.

Jenny replied, smiling and excited: 'I absolutely love it, I think it's wonderful.'

At that point, I didn't ask her to say yes. I just wanted her to think about it, to sow in her mind that Celebrate could be more than just family events; that under the banner of Celebrate we could run specific outreach programmes, using the Celebrate way of family, fellowship, and inclusiveness.

Despite Jenny's encouragement, I didn't move quickly: I was still in work earning good money in the City, funding my family, charities, and lifestyle. It took a further 18 months before I had the courage to take a leap of faith and seek permission from everyone involved in Celebrate, at a retreat held for weekend leaders at the end of January 2019.

With everyone on board, this left me with just a few months to plan everything before my planned launch date at the end of April.

And this was when God really started letting me know that his hand was on this mission.

Firstly, I had to be able to take three months off work. After qualifying and spending the first decade of my career as a civil engineer, I have worked in IT sales and development for more than 30 years. I had only been with my current employer for just over a year and didn't really fancy my chances of successfully securing a three-month sabbatical.

Six weeks ahead of the mission's start date I was called into my boss's office. He asked me to sit down and then, with watery eyes that looked like they might stream with tears at any moment, said: 'Russ, I have some terrible news for you. The company has decided that we need to lay some people off. I know your area is going really well, but I'm afraid we've decided that we're going to close that area down. '

I just burst out laughing. 'What? You think this is funny, do you?'

'No, no. Of course not, ' I said, still grinning from ear to ear. I explained to him the whole idea of the sailing mission, which he thought was tremendous, and that I was laughing because I had been struggling with how I was going to make it work - that I really needed some event to push me into doing this, and here we were.

Secondly, as well as needing the time off, I also needed money to fund the trip. I had already bought the boat – Mintaka, a Dufour 34 Performance cruiser racer sailing yacht – but I still needed the money for both the usual household expenses that until recently would have been covered by my salary, as well as funding the substantial expenses that come with being at sea for three months and mooring up next to some of the country's most famous waterside landmarks.

I had a small amount of redundancy money, but that wasn't going to cover it. I needed at least another £6,000. And this money couldn't come from any kind of fundraising, as all the funds we were raising on the trip were going to Joel's Bar, a Celebrate spin-off week for people in their late teens and early twenties, held every year at Worth Abbey in Sussex.

One idea I had was to earn some rental income by renovating an annexe to our house that has been occupied by Deirdre's father, who had sadly recently passed away. I started working from 7am in the morning until 10pm at night, painting and decorating, while at the same time trying to pull together the logistics for the trip.

I was becoming very tired and very stressed until, one day, the Lord said to me: 'You know that motorbike that you obsess about in the garage? It has got to go. '

Reluctantly, I said 'yes Lord ', and placed an advert for my pride and joy in Motorcycle News. The bike sold the same week at the full asking price, which is very unusual. That gave me £6,500, more than enough to fund the trip. It was uncanny how quick the bike sold.

This little episode of selling the bike, where I was obedient to the Lord and events unfolded rapidly, was an early sign of all that was to follow on this sailing pilgrimage.

However, despite the sale of the bike, I was still failing to learn the lesson that I don't need to do everything in my own strength. I continued to work all hours trying to decorate the annex to be able to rent it out, and plan the trip. This time it was Deirdre who intervened. One night, slumped in my chair after another grueling day, she said to me: 'This is ridiculous. I'm really supportive of you doing the trip, I think it's a great thing that you're doing. It's going to affect a lot of people. I think the Lord's behind it... I'm sure he's behind it. I'm with you. I want you to do it. Just forget about the money now because it's distracting you. You've sold the motorbike. Just stop now with the decorating and just focus on the trip and getting that sorted.'

I took Deirdre's advice, and from that point on the preparations sailed through. People started showing a real interest in my Facebook posts about my preparations, and I had all kinds of people, from all walks of life (mostly non sailors), contacting me and signing up to be part of the mission, either as crew on the boat, or to take part in the various Celebrate gatherings that would take place at quays and marinas around the country.

As the start of the mission neared, one sunny afternoon in early April I went down to the boat with Deirdre and my friend John. We raised the two flags that we would sail under for the whole trip, funded by my dear friend Sue Whitehead, who with her husband Charles was the founder of Celebrate. One of the flags displayed the Celebrate logo of a dove, and the other of the Celtic cross. This ancient symbol, which has the cross with a ring going through it, was the image the Lord gave to me of what we would be doing on this pilgrimage: creating a ring of prayer around the nation.

And as I sat there on the boat, the flags gently flapping in the breeze, I really started to feel that the Lord was behind this. He was now holding me through the preparations, and a sense of peace just came over me, a deep peace that I learnt on the trip seemed to accompany obedience. It showed me that if a direction is from God, no matter how arduous the task, I do not seem to get weary. Tired maybe, but not burdened, and I always find the energy to continue.

Having experienced this peace, having experienced so many small miracles during the preparation of the mission and events where the Lord seemed to be working in support of it, I couldn't believe it when Storm Hannah moved in.

'Surely not Lord, ' I asked. 'Surely I haven't got this wrong?' It made no sense to me. I had agreed pick-up locations for crew, gatherings around the country, and all of that looked like it was going to be blown off course by the storm.

Oh, ye of little faith! Over the course of Saturday evening the winds died down, and I was finally able to leave Hamble, near Southampton, with my first crew of Laura, Phil and Marcus Gower as we headed for our first stop at Brighton on Sunday morning. I kissed Deirdre farewell, waved to those family members, friends and well-wishers who had returned for this delayed send-off, and finally made our way down the chilly Solent in glorious sunshine on a 7knot reach. We rounded Selsey Bill through the Looe channel, dodging the numerous pot buoys, hoisted the spinnaker - the biggest of the boat's sails, set on a pole out from the mast - and sped away on a board reach at over 9 knots. Marcus, a sailor, was on the helm grinning like a Cheshire cat, watching the plumes of white sea foam coming out each side of the bow, while his mum Laura was playing guitar and singing songs of praise with husband Phil. We prayed and praised all the way along the South Coast, overlooked by the South Downs. Slightly delayed, but day one of this 77-day pilgrimage was finally underway.

As it turned out, the delay in departure was a real blessing: our original plan was to sail over to Brighton on Saturday afternoon, spend the night moored in the Marina, and have a gathering with some of the people from Celebrate Brighton on the Sunday morning. Due to the change in schedule, we instead arrived in Brighton on Sunday afternoon, and what was originally meant to be a small gathering of just a few people had grown to one similar in size to our send-off in Southampton the day before. If, as planned, we had the gathering on Sunday morning, many of these people would have been at church. Instead, Storm Hannah – or the Lord – held us back so that we could experience a far greater blessing at our first gathering.

Mintaka moored in Hamble, Southampton ready for our adventure

Some of the Celebrate Brighton team who turned up for our rearranged gathering

TWO

WHAT IF IT'S TRUE?
(BRIGHTON TO RAMSGATE)

Ask and it will be given to you;
seek and you will find;
knock and the door will be opened to you.
(Matthew chapter 7, verse 7)

EVERY BOAT HAS A NAME. IT IS A TRADITION THAT BEGAN OVER 1,000 years ago as a form of superstition: sailors would name their vessels after gods and goddesses, while Christians would name them after saints, all in the belief that these names would protect the boats on the open seas.

According to legend, every boat's name is recorded in the Ledger of the Deep, a record of boats' names held by Poseidon, the Greek god of the sea. To change a boat's name, boat owners must avoid Poseidon's wrath and ensure the original name is erased from his ledger by removing every single item on the boat bearing the original moniker - superstitious nonsense, but such are the rules of sailing.

The previous owner of the boat that I bought for the sailing mission had named it Mintaka. Like me, they clearly liked looking heavenwards: Mintaka is one of the three stars on Orion's belt. It is actually a binary star, comprising two stars that closely rotate around each other every five days, but appear to the naked eye as one. I like the symbolism of their close relationship because that to me is what life is all about.

While it would have been nice to have a more appropriately named boat for this pilgrimage – even if it was just a saint's name - I was loath to go through the costly process of dumping every bit of kit that had Mintaka written on it, the onboard Emergency Position Indicating Radio Beacons and re-registering the boat with the Small Ship Registry just to rename her.

Instead, I decided that in addition to the two flags of the Celebrate dove and Celtic cross, I wanted to make the boat visible by sticking a slogan across the sides of the boat that could be easily seen as we sailed into many of the towns and cities on our trip.

As I thought about sailing around the country, going into very secular environments, I didn't want to put something on the boat that was just shouting out a belief. I wanted something that might spark a conversation.

It came to me very quickly to have the words 'What if it's true?' emblazoned across the sides. I wanted to say to people: 'I've got something that's true for me, what's true for you? What's the 'it' in your life? Is it the football club that you support and if your team is up, so are you, and if they're down then you're down too? Or is it the sports car sitting in the garage that is your pride and joy? Is that the big joy in your life? And if so, is it true? What is it delivering for you? Is it completely delivering the joy and happiness that you want out of life? There are many wonderful things in life, but in themselves do they really satisfy you? '

Some people might respond by saying, 'Oh, I don't believe in anything. ' But even responses like that prompt the question: 'Perhaps there is something that I should believe in? '

Having agreed this slogan with Jenny and the Celebrate leadership team, I had it made up in large vinyl letters saying, '*What if it's true?*' in two-feet-high blue lettering. This dwarfed 'Mintaka' at the fore of the boat, and was the cause of much confusion as we sailed into some of the world's busiest ports and controlled seaways.

Between 500 and 600 ships pass through the Dover Strait in the English Channel every day, making it the busiest shipping channel in the world. The Port of Dover, meanwhile, is one of the world's busiest passenger terminals, and sits next to the marina where we wanted to put in for the second night of the mission. Keeping every boat and ship moving in Dover is a harbour master who is more like an air traffic controller. He and his team - known as Vessel Traffic Service (VTS) - use a combination of maritime tracking systems, radio and video cameras to control movements in and out of the port.

I radioed the harbour master asking for permission to come into the marina.

'I've got three ferries coming out, you just stay where you are,' came the reply. We waited.

'Okay, go. Come in, and I'll direct you exactly to where I want you to go. '

I pushed the engine's throttle and started moving the boat towards the marina. Suddenly a panicked voice came on the radio: 'Boat 'What if it's true' 'What if it's true' please state your intentions! '

The boat that the harbour master has given permission to come into the marina is listed on the marine tracking system as Mintaka, but he was now picking up on his video screens what looked like a boat called 'What if it's true' heading towards one of the world's busiest passenger ferry terminals with no permission. The harbour master was calling out 'What if it's true' on radio channel 16, the international channel for calling and distress messages. By law every boat must keep this channel open, so every boat within a 25-mile radius of the world's busiest shipping lane - with hundreds of seamen monitoring the VHF - was now listening to the words 'What if it's true, what if it's true ' being repeated, over and over again across the radio.

My reply was to assure VTS that we were indeed Mintaka, and 'What if it's true' was just a slogan on the side of the boat. It wasn't the kind of conversation I had in mind when I chose 'What if it's true' as a slogan, but it certainly was a message that was already reaching the masses!

This fraught passage into Dover marina was the first overnight stop for my new crewmates Paul and Veronica Langford, who had joined me in Brighton earlier that day.

Having sailed with my first crew of Laura, Phil and Marcus Gower from Southampton on Sunday, I arrived at Brighton's marina, which is about a mile down the coast from the town's famous stony beach and pier. The Gowers had arranged a lift back to Southampton with two friends who weren't particularly religious, and we invited them onboard to have dinner with us before that evening's praise gathering. Over dinner, discussions soon turned into prayer. This was the first instance of the boat becoming a haven of prayer for anyone who stepped aboard.

And the prayer levels were about to reach another level with Paul and Veronica joining the crew. I hadn't met the Langfords previously, having only discussed the trip and the logistics with them via Facebook and email. They had told me that while they weren't sailors, a trip of this kind was on their 'bucket list ' of things they wanted to do as a couple. And having prayed about it, they wanted to spend a whole week with me, sailing all the way from Brighton to London.

I met them after dinner on the Sunday, Paul bringing his guitar to help lead the music as 20 or so of us praised and worshipped together at the marina that first night, engaging with onlookers, and praying with some of the people around us - it seemed so natural, like we do this every week.

The next morning, on my own with them, it became clear that I was in the presence of a deeply prayerful couple. Like every Christian who was to sail with me on this trip, the Langfords brought their own prayer life on to the boat. This was a form of constant praying, using Magnificat to guide that prayer throughout the day. Named after Mary's prayer of thanksgiving in the first chapter of Luke's Gospel, Magnificat is a magazine that gives daily and morning prayers based on the Catholic Church's Liturgy of the Hours. It also provides prayers based on the scriptures read at Mass each day. It wasn't a form of prayer that I was used to, but Paul and Veronica were praying this throughout the day, and I joined in. In between this we were singing songs of worship aided by Paul's guitar.

Paul and Veronica placed everything in prayer. As we went along the coast, they prayed for problems like drug addiction in many of these English seaside towns that they knew so well. With such a faithful and relentless approach to prayer, I'm not sure why I was surprised that, when I revealed an oversight in my planning for this trip, they suggested we take it to the Lord. I confessed to them that I hadn't managed to source or make a fender board for the boat. A fender board is a long plank of wood with holes drilled through it to accommodate captive ropes, looped through so that it can hang over the side of the boat. You can't buy fender boards – they must be made. I was concerned that our lack of a fender board would limit the number of the places we could go into: as we went away from the south there would be fewer marinas, and the most common harbours would be old fishing quays. My lovely white plastic boat wasn't capable of going up against the rough piles and stone walls of these fishing quays. It needed a fender board to rub against the wall, securing purchase against its rough surface and protecting the boat.

I told Paul and Veronica that it was really bothering me that I didn't have one.

'Well, you've got to pray about it, ' said Veronica.

I responded with some doubt, slipping out of prayer mode and into my old ways of being a pragmatic engineer and sailor. I said, 'I suppose so ', while actually thinking 'or I could just miss out the lovely old harbours '.

After Brighton and the successful if fraught entry into Dover marina, our next stop was further along the Kent coast at Ramsgate.

We reached Ramsgate after successfully sailing past Goodwin Sands, which in previous centuries has been the site of many shipwrecks, but today is better known for the seals that lounge on the sands and are occasionally gobbled up by passing Orca whales.

Paul, Veronica and I moored up in Ramsgate's marina, and started walking along the pontoon. There was a crowd of people dressed in old-fashioned sailing clothing – the crews of six or seven boats, all dressed in retro gear like tweed jackets, caps and corduroy trousers. It was a chilly April evening, but they were all sat out on the pontoon around a few small candles and a keg of what turned out to be rum.

This was my first experience of what it felt like to interact with people having spent all day in prayer. It is difficult to explain, but you give off an energy that is just, well, attractive. When someone has a great joy in them, when they have a big smile and a great energy, you're drawn towards them, you want to find out what makes them tick.

Inevitably we found ourselves in the middle of these time-travelling sailors, who turned out to be eccentrics from the Netherlands. They explained that their trip was a tradition, and we told them about our mission. It was the ideal first opportunity to say, 'we're praying with people ', and they invited us to pray for their protection.

After the conversation, rum and prayer, we left them and walked on up the gangway from the pontoon to use the marina's facilities.

At the top there was a skip, and I had to duck to avoid a large plank of wood that was sticking out of it. I did a double-take and couldn't believe my eyes: it was a fender board! Sticking out of the skip so I couldn't miss it was a perfect piece of timber: teak, about six foot long, one foot wide, and two inches thick.

I pulled it out, a bit weather-worn but other than that it was in perfect working condition. Veronica had been speaking to a man down on the pontoon who was varnishing two beautiful new fender boards next to his lovely old wooden boat. I walked down to him.

'Is this yours? ' I asked, holding the fender board.

'Yeah. '

'Is it alright if we have it. '

'Of course you can, I've thrown it away. '

I'm not sure what he thought of me, laughing and then catching up with Veronica to hug her - all over an old piece of wood. I couldn't believe it, and just as in my boss' office, chuckled with incredulity at God's providence.

'Surely it can't be this easy, ' I thought. 'Is this a joke Lord? We just pray for something and it happens? '

'What if it's true', indeed. The fender board was to be the first of many answers to prayer on this pilgrimage.

CREW TESTIMONY
PAUL LANGFORD

Early in January 2019 I wrote a list of things I want to do in my life - the fun things. One was to sail in a yacht and even simply to sleep aboard one. I had been sailing dinghies for years, which is something I love, but the thought of a proper voyage attracted me enough to be at the top of the list. Imagine my delight, and Veronica's enthusiasm on my behalf, when the Celebrate sailing mission was announced. Our first day was spent sailing past our home in Saltdean and our beloved beach hut, waters we had kayaked and swam in with many different friends. It was gorgeous weather for April, with just enough breeze to keep us sailing. We were a little way past Beachy Head and the iconic lighthouse when out of the corner of my eye I saw the dark silent shape of a creature dipping below the water. We were amongst a pod of dolphins gently diving and fishing the Beachy Head reef!

Our second day, from Eastbourne to Dover, was a long trek: cold at first, and with a swell that made Veronica seasick. Around midday it became sunny and Mintaka rushed along, heeled over so the cabin windows were touching the bright green water as it swept past. Again, we saw a dolphin. Helming Mintaka as she sped along, pitching to the waves, was glorious.

We were there with Russ to pray and support him and the mission in any way we could, it was a joyful time and every conversation at a mooring led to witnessing.

The time onboard grew my faith through the continuous sense of being 'on mission'. I loved the fact that when we stopped anywhere, we would naturally fall into conversations with people along the lines of 'where are you going?' This was such a gift for witnessing. We made a habit of praying together throughout the day, and it was beautiful to be out in the elements of sea and wind where God's creation was so much bigger than our man-made world. Seeing the pod of dolphins swimming around us, it felt like the Lord was really loving me and blessing me personally.

CREW TESTIMONY
VERONICA LANGFORD

From the moment I thought of joining the mission, I felt a passionate desire to be part of the journey up the Thames into London, praying for the city and the nation. I know it was a move of God that I so wanted to join the mission, it was not natural for me to want to put myself in the way of seasickness and being out of my depth, quite literally! I was delighted with Russ' suggestion on the first morning that I steer Mintaka out of the marina and onto the open sea, thinking – wow, we are really doing this thing!

The voyage had countless special moments: watching the coastline slip past, noting beautiful places like St Margaret's Bay, seeing the makeup of the coast changing, enjoying mugs of tea and Russ' scooby doo-style sandwiches (thanks go to Deirdre who ensured Mintaka was so richly stocked with provisions). So many highlights come to mind: gulls lifting off the water as we approached, whoops of delight at seeing the dolphins off Beachy Head, the lovely quay at Ramsgate.

Regarding the fender board – I just felt quite intuitively when Russ said he needed one that we should pray specifically and ask for one, so I did and thought no more of it. Soon after, when I was walking along the pontoon, I met a man doing some work on his boat. I talked with him briefly and much to my delight later found out from Russ that he was the provider of the much-needed fender board. He had been varnishing the new one, whilst his old one was waiting for Russ to discover it in the skip. Such sweet provision! I was delighted by Russ' reaction and it highlighted to me the need to be specific in prayer and that our Father really knows what our needs are. Some things we pray for over months and years and we are still waiting to see the answer, but on this occasion it was rapid response!

Captain Russ at the helm

Navigating the world's busiest shipping channel at sunset

THREE

EBB AND FLOW
(RAMSGATE TO LONDON)

'O precious is the flow
that makes me white as snow;
no other fount I know;
nothing but the blood of Jesus.'
(*Robert Lowry*)

HEADING NORTH FROM RAMSGATE BY BOAT, YOU ARE VERY
quickly out of the English Channel and into the North Sea.
I was to spend two weeks in its biting winds, experiencing
some of the mission's toughest sailing conditions but also visiting
holy sites and seeing an abundance of wildlife.

Paul and Veronica, meanwhile, were to experience the North Sea
just briefly: instead of heading north from the Kent coast up to
Essex, we headed west after Margate and into the Thames Estuary
towards London, where they would leave me.

You must choose your moment when deciding to sail up the
Thames. At over 200 miles it is the UK's longest river, with
ferocious ebb and flood tides. The flood tide is this mighty tide that
sweeps into London, and you cannot go into the city unless you
take the tide – it is just too strong. You must get yourself in position
on the Isle of Sheppey, consult tide tables, and be ready to go with
the flow of the flood tide when it comes. We did so while moored
up at Queenborough, a small town on the western side of the Isle

of Sheppey, and at the mouth of the Thames. We had some time to kill before we could sail in on the flood tide, so I took the opportunity to go on my first bike ride of the trip. Like sailing and motorbikes, bicycles are another passion of mine, and I was able to squeeze a folding bike on to the boat.

Cycling around Queenborough was like riding through a microcosm of the history of the Thames itself: cobbled streets gave way to paved roads, and buildings ran the gamut from Tudor cottages through to Georgian townhouses, Victorian villas, and 1950s semis.

Queenborough also has its fair share of industrial facilities near the water, but the activity at its docks is just a fraction of what it was in the past. Today they seem to mainly serve as a holding pen for new cars being imported and exported to and from Europe, which line Sheppey's coast from Queenborough up to Sheerness at the top of the Isle.

However, in the past Queenborough was a strategic port, located as it is both at the mouth of the Thames and where the Swale meets the Medway. It is also – a rare and precious thing with tidal rivers – possible to land at Queenborough at any tide. It first became a port of note in medieval times, when King Edward III built a fort there to guard safe passage of ships down the Swale during the Hundred Years War. He named the town after his wife, Queen Philippa, and it soon became a major hub for the wool trade, one of the major money-spinners for the Crown during the many costly wars with France. From this high point, Queenborough's fortunes varied over the centuries, including going bankrupt, and several days in the 17th century when the Dutch invaded it. After experiencing a depression in the 1850s, Queenborough's fortunes revived in the Victorian era when the railway came to the town. Glass, cement, timber and even coal-washing became vibrant industries in Queenborough. Today, however, those industries have largely disappeared and, like many coastal towns up and down the country, it suffered for much of the 20th century. Property prices are so low that in 2019 Queenborough was named the number one place to buy a house in South East England; the lack of economic activity in past decades means it still retains much of its olde-worlde charm, with a beach to boot, making it something of a bargain in property investors' eyes.

After cycling around Queenborough, praying for its residents and an economic revival, I returned to the boat, reuniting with Paul and Veronica.

For both of them, waiting here at Queenborough meant praying and contemplating what would be the culmination of their trip: London. For Veronica, this journey up the Thames would be a return to her hometown, and the realisation of her own vision for the mission.

Veronica's was the most thorough of any enquiry I received about joining me on this trip: she was so keen to do it that she sent me a five-page CV of all her sailing exploits, covering every time she had been on the water – even her times on a rowing boat as a little girl.

I phoned her and said: 'Veronica, you needn't have sent me all that - I can sail the boat solo, it will just be great that you're there.'

'I was just desperate to come,' she replied, going on to explain her vision, which knitted together her faith, her London childhood and her career as a nurse. Veronica's vision was this: that the mighty tide that she looked at for years sweeping into London, was like the Lord's precious blood coming into the city. Because as blood flows in, it brings with it the nutrients that our bodies need. For London it meant the Lord coming in with his blessing into the city, building the churches, building the youth and really bringing about a Holy Spirit transformation.

But the Thames tide also comes out as ferociously as it goes in, and Veronica's vision went on: after the Blood has done its work bringing the nutrients, it takes all the discharged carbon dioxide away. It would cleanse London of knife crime, cleanse it of relationship problems, cleanse it of things that were going on that were not of the Lord and drag it back out on the ebb tide out to Sea.

Veronica wanted to come into London on the tide, praying as best she could and, once she had arrived, pray that all that was not of the Lord would be taken back out on the ebb tide.

As we sailed in on the flood tide, the constant prayer that Veronica, Paul and I had been immersed in for the past seven days since Brighton intensified, changing from the reading of

Magnificat and a general resting in the Lord's presence to a more fervent taking hold of his promises and declaring them over the Capital, home to eight million people. All this prayer was changing me, and mostly for the better. However, the build up to London and our growing expectation of what was to come when we gathered with our Celebrate family at Tower Hill might also explain the momentary lapse of concentration that almost cost us dearly.

We had reached London a day early – I wanted to make sure we were up the Thames before a forecast storm blew in. I had booked a prominent place in the marina at St Katharine's Docks, next to Tower Bridge for the Celebrate gathering the next day. Mooring at such an iconic location isn't cheap, so I opted to spend our extra night ahead of the gathering somewhere more affordable.

A mile downstream on the south bank of the Thames, between Rotherhithe and Deptford, is the South Dock Marina, one of the many former docks spread across East London. In all my time sailing, I have never encountered so many large docks in such a relatively small space. The traffic on the Thames in east London at its prime, in the Victorian and Pre-War eras, must have been something to behold. But after heavy bombing in the Second World War and the opening of the Port of Tilbury in Essex, close to the M25, freight traffic largely disappeared from this part of London. Today, those docks that haven't been filled in for commercial developments like Canary Wharf serve only as moorings for recreational and residential boats.

How freight boats and barges were ever expected to get into an entrance like the one at South Dock Marina is beyond me. It is just five metres at its widest point, encased by large concrete walls on either side. With the Thames ripping past it, it was impossible to sail straight in. With the motor running, I approached the entrance at a 45-degree angle, and at the last moment before the bow hit the far wall, I had to flip out the back of the boat to motor straight in.

As we entered the Marina it became clear that we had entered a little village on the water, with almost every vessel there a houseboat. The owner of the water-borne home we moored next to told us his boat had proud history: it was one of the 700 civilian vessels that rescued more than 330,000 British, French and Belgian troops from Dunkirk in June 1940 after being surrounded by advancing German forces. In his famous, 'We shall fight them on the beaches' speech in the House of Commons after the rescue mission, Winston Churchill hailed Dunkirk as a 'miracle of deliverance'. This felt like an appropriate place to be moored up for the night.

As we stepped out onto the pontoon, we found ourselves in the heart of a wonderful community. Everyone we met went out of his or her way to help us – this was not the London I had experienced in my many years of commuting to the city by train. It was evident that there was something special about entering cities by water.

Paul and Veronica's daughter Sasha lived nearby and joined us

for dinner. After dinner we did the same thing that we had
done every night so far in the pilgrimage while the Langfords
were aboard: we went for a prayer walk. These walks were a
chance to thank the Lord for the place that we were in, ask him
to bless it, and to offer prayer to anyone we encountered. That
night – as I was to discover in all the big towns and cities we
visited – many of those we encountered were homeless. We took
the time to sit with them, listen to them, hear their story, and
finally offer them prayer and a few quid.

The next morning, we headed up the Thames to St. Katharine's
Dock. And this is where the excitement of reaching the pinnacle
of Paul and Veronica's trip almost proved very costly.

In many ways, when it comes to the simple mechanics of sailing
a boat, I can do it easier on my own than with novice sailors
for passengers. If I ask a novice to do something, I then must
check it is done correctly. However, in the excitement of arriving
in St Katharine's Dock, being greeted at the quayside by
Charles and Sue Whitehead – the founders of the original Celebrate conference in Ilfracombe – I forgot that Paul and Veronica
were novice sailors.

We had turned into the entrance for St. Katharine's Dock, which
comes just before the iconic Tower Bridge. I had asked for a
prestigious mooring place in the marina, which put us just on
the left by the entrance. Surprisingly it wasn't too busy, so after
going through two locks to get into the marina, I pulled a nice
manoeuvre to bring us next to the harbour wall on the starboard

side, with the bow facing back towards the lock gates. Paul, Veronica and I jumped ashore to exchange hugs with Charles and Sue when, suddenly, a gust of wind caught the boat and it started moving away from the quayside. I had failed to check Paul and Veronica's knots and suddenly the ropes keeping it tethered to the side came loose. Mintaka's bow, with anchor sticking out, was now heading like a battering ram straight for the side of a very expensive and very new-looking French yacht. 'No!' I shouted, and two men on board the French boat saw what was happening. They dived down to hang over the side of their boat to stop Mintaka's impact with their arms. After much embarrassment and sincere apologies, I rescued the boat from them, taking it back to its mooring, this time making sure it was firmly tied in place. The whole episode was a timely reminder, in a far more controlled environment than the open seas, that I could not and should not take anything for granted while sailing on this mission. I was to face far greater sailing challenges in the weeks and months ahead, and I needed to remember to check and double-check: I was responsible for the boat and its novice crew.

Later that day, despite the rain that came with the storm that had blown in, we had a great gathering. Around 40 people, old and young, associated with Joel's Bar and the Celebrate weekends in Twickenham and St. Albans, turned up for a time of soggy praise and worship in view of Tower Bridge. Deirdre was among them, London being the first of only three towns where she would visit me during the mission. It was, of course, wonderful to see her again, if not a bit surreal as my two worlds of life-on-the-boat and life-at-home came together. Undeterred by the rain showers, most of us sang praise loudly while a few others prayed with passersby, including a couple being photographed on their wedding day, which was a joy. With elevated spirits we ended our quayside gathering by all moving to a nearby pub to dry ourselves out and continue the celebration.

The next morning was a Sunday and my final morning with Paul and Veronica, so we headed to mass at the nearby English Martyrs church. We entered the church in the spirit of effortless prayerfulness that we had shared for the past week on the boat. Straight after the mass had finished, Veronica turned around to the lady sitting behind her and offered her prayer. She was a Polish lady, a teacher at a nearby school. Veronica laid her hands on her and prayed for the healing of her back pain.

Inspired by Veronica, Paul and I started to move around the church offering prayer to others.

At this point the priest walked over asking who we were and what we were doing offering prayer ministry unannounced in his church.

We explained about the mission, and he said: 'Can you pray for me? I'm a counsellor and I'm about to head out to Sri Lanka to help those who have suffered from the bombings.'

Just two weeks earlier, on Sunday 21st April 2019 – Easter Sunday – three churches across Sri Lanka and three hotels in its capital Colombo were bombed by Islamist terrorists, killing 277 people and injuring hundreds more. Father Edmund Reginald told us he was in training as a counsellor. He hailed from Sri Lanka's northern Tamil region, where communities were still trying to recover from 25 years of civil war, which ended in 2009. Father Edmund was in London to learn the necessary skills to be able to minister to the many Catholics who had suffered during the civil war. However, following the bombings across the country, he was now taking a break from his studies and heading home to comfort his brothers and sisters in Christ.

After some prayer for him and for the victims of the bombings, Father Edmund asked if he could come back to the boat with us. It was a wonderful way to end my last day with Paul and Veronica: with a priest blessing our boat and our mission, and us in turn blessing him and his vital work.

CREW TESTIMONY
VERONICA LANGFORD

The thought of sailing up the Thames into London, praying for our capital city and our nation was something that attracted me powerfully. I realised when I heard about this mission that I urgently wanted to do it, and I knew God had planted this desire in my spirit long before the invitation came. We even had a jigsaw model of Tower Bridge on our mantelpiece that felt like a sign of what was to come. I felt an irrepressible joy about going on the mission despite a history of seasickness – that must have been God! As we sailed inland from the mouth of the Thames estuary, I felt this strong desire to pray and prophesy at the bow of the yacht over London and the nation.

We passed under the Queen Elizabeth Bridge and later through the Thames Barrier with its huge structures shaped like the iron on our ironing board. Coming into the city was amazing, with the skyscrapers around us and the Millennium Dome appearing to port.

As I prayed at the front of the boat, I felt a spiritual charge of certainty within me, inspiring me to intercede for our capital, our government and our nation. I prayed for the return of the King of Kings, and for the cleansing and renewing life in his precious blood, like a spiritual artery flowing to the heart of the nation.

I had an image of a royal ship with a red sail marked with a golden crown, which was coming up the river to the heart of the city. At the end of our voyage as we left the Mintaka, we saw Tower Bridge open and a large historic Thames barge with red sails go upstream to the heart of the city – God's timing is perfect, and he is in the detail!

Motoring through the Thames Barrier and into London with Paul and Veronica

FOUR

PETER'S CALL
(LONDON TO LOWESTOFT)

'As Jesus walked beside the Sea of Galilee, he saw Simon
and his brother Andrew casting a net into the lake,
for they were fishermen. 'Come, follow me,' Jesus said,
'and I will send you out to fish for people.'
At once they left their nets and followed him.'
(Mark chapter 1, verses 16-18)

THERE WERE SEVERAL SPIRITUALLY SIGNIFICANT ITEMS THAT I carried with me on the boat for the journey. The item that most people were likely to encounter during the pilgrimage was the mission prayer scroll. It is a long white sheet of acrylic with two wooden ends, made for me by my son-in-law Dan in his wood-turning class. Printed on the scroll were all the prayers offered by the teams that run the various Celebrate weekends around the UK, and we would pray these at every quayside gathering across the country, to elevate the petitions and help to give people a greater sense of Celebrate as a nationwide movement rather than just their own regional weekend event.

Another item that I carried was a small cross, made by Palestinian Christians from vines in the Hebron Valley. I had picked this up during a trip to the Holy Land six months earlier, where I also found the third and final spiritual item that I carried throughout the mission with me: a small stone from Capernaum.

Located on the north shore of the Sea of Galilee, Capernaum was a fishing village that existed from the second century before Christ to the 11th century AD. It was the base for the majority of Jesus' ministry, with Matthew going so far as referring to it as 'the Lord's own town' (Matthew 9:1). All the Gospels cite the town as one where Jesus spent time teaching and performing miracles, including the healing of Peter's mother-in-law, which in Mark and Luke's Gospels comes after Jesus has been teaching in Capernaum's synagogue.

It is also considered the hometown of many of the disciples, including Matthew, brothers James and John, Andrew and his brother Peter.

After sailing on the Sea of Galilee, our pilgrimage group was taken to the ruins believed to once have been Peter's house in Capernaum. Many think this is the place Jesus stayed during his Galilean ministry. Franciscan archaeologists excavated it in 1968, also discovering the remains of a house church and a later Byzantine church on the same site. The Franciscans have since built a modern spaceship-looking church that now hovers over the site.

What really struck me about the place was how close to the water it was, and how so much of Jesus ministry was spent going from town to town by boat, even to the point of getting in a boat to teach the large crowds gathered at the shore.

So I picked up this stone at the shore by Peter's house, knowing this may well have been the spot where Jesus asked Peter to follow him, promising to make him and Andrew 'fishers of men'.

Holding the stone, looking out over Galilee as the water lapped gently against the shore, it occurred to me that Jesus didn't call Peter to follow him when he was teaching in the synagogue. Jesus came to where Peter was, to his place of work, right into the middle of his ordinary daily life. Peter would have been there on the boat by the shore, preparing the nets, and Jesus entered his environment, meeting him where he was, on his terms.

Every day that little stone from the shore at Capernaum reminded me that, following Jesus' example, this mission was about going out of church and meeting people where they are. As it happened, this was an easy thing to do on a sailing pilgrimage. Because when you sail into a harbour, you come right into the heart of a community. This is a community made up of boat owners and sailors, commercial and amateur fisher-men, and all the people around the quayside and in its pubs. And these are all people of the sea, people who want to know your story when you sail into the middle of their community.

It was completely different to my past experiences of evangel-ising. Deirdre and I take part in the Healing on the Streets ministry in Southampton. We set up our little table with a flag and two chairs in the middle of Bitterne's suburban post-war shopping precinct. As we sit there people walk past and we try

---

to engage them and offer prayer, but invariably we get met with the gesture of a lifted palm and 'no thank you, not interested, it's not for me'. But in that situation, I've got no relationship with these people. It's a cold call and I have no right to speak to them.

From day one, my experience on the sailing mission was completely different. Arriving at harbours and marinas, we were welcomed by people who considered us part of their community: we were all people of the sea together. So often people were as eager to find out about what I was doing as I was to tell them about the pilgrimage. Bonds are formed and connections are made easily at the quayside, because you're all in it together, braving the sea and helping each other out. For example, a boat would come in just after me, and I'd jump off my boat and rush over to another part of the marina, grabbing their line to help them to come ashore. Or a boat would sail in with a foreign flag on it, and I could help the crew by telling them how to get connected in the marina, letting them know where to go and where to get provisions from.

These simple acts of kindness formed bonds that then made conversation effortless. We would ask each other where we were from, where we were each going, and the conversation would soon turn to what we were doing on the mission. And I would say to them: 'I'm putting this ring of prayer around the United Kingdom, but we're praying for people as we go as well...is there anything I can pray for you?'

Within a minute of such discussions, we were praying with

people. People were open to being prayed with, in a way that they never are when we offer Healing on the Streets in Bitterne. Somehow the Lord seemed to have already prepared certain people and showed us who to approach.

And it wasn't just fellow sailors either: we would go into the quayside pubs frequented by all sorts of nautical types, and they wanted to hear our stories. Again, very quickly, we would be praying for them.

Like Jesus did with Peter, we simply met people where they were, on their terms, and we were able to make the kinds of connections that sometimes just aren't possible with more overt forms of evangelisation. We were also able, with locals in particular, to offer a follow-up to the prayer by telling them about the Celebrate gathering that we would be having and put them in touch with people who could tell them more about church activity in their area.

As well as acting as a great focal point in our outreach, the Celebrate gatherings also helped me form relationships with a very special group of people: the harbourmasters. When it came to visiting big cities on this trip, I didn't want the gatherings to be hidden away in out-of-town marinas. I wanted to be in the heart of these cities, moored up in ceremonial quays. So as well as visiting St. Katherine's Docks, right underneath Tower Bridge, I wanted to moor up in places like the Welsh Assembly Government building in Cardiff and the Barbican in Plymouth. While anyone can rock up at a marina, you need special access and privileges to moor up at the places where I wanted to hold Celebrate gatherings. So, as I planned the trip, I made regular phone calls to harbourmasters up and down the length and breadth of Britain.

When I explained what I was doing, it was clear that this wasn't the kind of requests they were used to dealing with, and I ended up building a close rapport with many of them. They embraced the novelty of my request, saying that they thought it was a good thing for us to do: raising money for Joel's Bar's work with teenagers and young adults, putting a ring of prayer around the country and coming into their city praying for its prosperity, praying for their schools and their public services.

After leaving London, we headed for Ipswich, the city of our next quayside ceremonial gathering supported by folk from Celebrate East Anglia. Having said farewell to Paul and Veronica, I was joined on the leg out of London by Tim Stevens, part of the fabric of Celebrate, and Zoe Lavery, a young mother and Celebrate newbie who was keen to get more involved. They sailed with me only for a short while, up the Thames - stopping at Queenborough again - and out along the Essex coast. The sailing was so peaceful, with clear skies and a fair breeze, and the three of us had a thoroughly joyful time together. I was sad to wave goodbye to Tim and Zoe at Brightlingsea: this was the start of a continual pattern of making new friends, saying good-bye with little time to reflect, before meeting the new crew for the start of their adventure.

The new crew at Brightlingsea were Kevin Pugh and Catherine Hankard, who were joining me for just one day. After creeping out of the shallow creek in the small hours of the early morning, we popped up the spinnaker flown by Catherine, who had never sailed before, and zipped along the Essex coast. After clearing the busy container port of Felixstowe, we headed inland up the surprisingly beautiful River Orwell, sailing all the way up this 12-mile river into Ipswich. I had agreed with the harbour master that I could moor up in the quay by its historic Isaac Lord buildings. With some parts dating back as early 1400, these buildings were part of the merchant's quarter when Ipswich was a prosperous trading town, used both as a maltings and as a place where corn, wool, and coal were sold. Today they are a huge complex of multiple bars, and the busiest spot on the waterside. It was the ideal location for our Celebrate gathering to take place and give witness. Celebrate East Anglia takes place in Bury St. Edmunds, 27 miles northwest of Ipswich, so we had people from across the region come and join us at the waterfront. We sang songs of praise, but we didn't just stay in a holy huddle. After the singing, we started walking around the quayside and in the bars offering prayer. These walkabouts were becoming a daily occurrence on this mission, and what was becoming clear was that there was a surprising openness and appetite for prayer among many. I lost count of the number of times a person would refuse prayer for themselves, but then in the same breath ask us to pray for one of their loved ones.

This pilgrimage was teaching me a new kind of vulnerability, a willingness to look stupid or be considered a fool by others while doing the Lord's work. It would also soon remind me that social interactions weren't the only way I was making myself vulnerable on this trip.

Kevin and Catherine were to be my last shipmates for nearly a week. After Ipswich I would spend the next six days of the mission sailing solo. I planned it this way, as to remain on schedule I needed to put in long days at sea, and I felt this would be too arduous for novice crew. I headed further up the coast towards Lowestoft, the most easterly town in the United Kingdom. The weather was already sending me warnings of what was to come in the next 24 hours, with unforecast 30-knot winds blowing me about on the Orwell, causing me to wait on a buoy at the Suffolk Yacht Club before attempting to press on with the 50-mile leg around East Anglia to Lowestoft, which ended up being a fast blast under spinnaker. It was the eleventh night of the pilgrimage and my first on my own, although I wouldn't be without company for very long: I was due to meet up the next day with Deirdre, who had arranged to be in the area visiting her elderly uncle Terry and aunt Celia in the hope of catching up with me.

That morning, before they arrived, I had to get the boat's Automatic Identification System (AIS) fixed. This tracking system was being used by many of the mission's supporters to track my progress, and for the last few days I had been receiving messages via the mission's Facebook page that the boat was not showing on AIS tracking websites. More importantly, a functioning AIS system allows other vessels to see me, keeping me safe while sailing in fog or through the night.

With help from marina staff I quickly got in touch with two local marine electronics specialists, Kevin and Glenn, who were able to fix the system for me. Yet again I was bowled over by the generosity and kindness of strangers: both men dropped everything they were doing to come and help me, and then when I explained what I was doing and how I was raising money for Joel's Bar, they refused to charge me for their time.

Deirdre arrived with uncle Terry and aunt Celia, and I gave them a quick tour of the boat before we all went to lunch. It was a brief reunion with my wife: after the meal I said farewell to Celia and Terry and kissed Deirdre goodbye, before once again hopping aboard Mintaka. I was now headed for Grimsby, where we would have the next gathering for Celebrate Cleethorpes.

Soon after heading out of Lowestoft, I spotted a massive angry black cloud alongside me. It was hovering over Great Yarmouth. I hoped it would stay inland and I could skirt past it. But almost as soon as I thought this, the cloud swept out instantly and a 40 knot-plus squall smashed into the boat, flipping it around 180 degrees so I was now facing south instead of north. The rain was horizontal, and dark as night, and I struggled to get the sail down, worrying that it might snap the mast. Little by little I clawed the sail down enough for it to stop catching wind. I then just ran the boat before the wind and allowed it to blow through. This vicious squall lasted for roughly 30 minutes.

I had planned for this solo leg of the trip between Ipswich, Grimsby and Newcastle to be one where I sailed for up to 20 hours at a time, covering hundreds of miles each day. This storm so soon into my solo leg reminded me how vulnerable I was, out here on my own in the open sea. But I still felt at peace, trusting in my capability, the boat and God.

When the storm had passed and I was able to hoist the sail and begin moving forwards once again, I reflected on how being vulnerable is so essential to growing in faith. We must move into areas where we are uncertain about the outcome, where we have to - as St. Paul puts it - 'walk by faith, not sight'. We must be like Peter: just as he stepped out of the boat and walked towards Jesus on the water. We have to move out of our comfort zones to meet the Lord in the places he is calling us to. This means following Jesus' example and meeting others where they are, even if that means going to places where we feel uncomfortable and vulnerable.

Celebrate East Anglia gathering in the heart of Ipswich

Kevin and Glenn,
who fixed the tracking system

Being blown about on the North Sea

FIVE

LEARNING TO ANCHOR
(LOWESTOFT TO LINDISFARNE)

'In every high and stormy gale,
My anchor holds within the veil'
(Edward Mote/Hillsong)

THERE ARE MORE THAN 250 PUBS IN THE UK WITH ANCHOR IN their name, ranging from the straightforward 'The Anchor', to the regal 'Crown & Anchor' and, my favourite, 'The Hope & Anchor', which is a reference to this line from the sixth chapter of the Letter to the Hebrews:

> *This hope we have as an anchor of the soul, a hope both sure and steadfast and one which enters within the veil, where Jesus has entered as a forerunner for us, having become a high priest forever according to the order of Melchizedek. (Hebrews 6:19-20)*

For such an iconic part of the boat, intimately tied up with the identity of this seafaring nation and a biblical metaphor for steadfast faith, I was embarrassingly inexperienced when it came to using an anchor.

On the south coast we are blessed with an abundance of marinas, and visitors' buoys in the bays. It is quite easy to spend your days cruising around the Solent, over to the Isle of Wight - maybe even taking part in a race - before mooring up in another marina and doing it all again the next day. You don't need to use an anchor when mooring in a marina; you simply need to tie the lines to the pontoon. As a result, if, like me, you do most of your sailing around somewhere like Southampton, whole weeks, summers and years can pass without ever needing to use the anchor.

This was a problem, because on this trip I wanted to go to places where there would be no marinas and I would need to be able to anchor.

I planned for the first of these places to be the Farne Islands and the Holy Island of Lindisfarne, on the north-eastern corner of England's coast. Just as with the fender board, I had failed to do anything in the way of preparation, never having used Mintaka's anchor before. And so, leaving it until the last minute, I found myself playing with the anchor one calm, sunny morning while moored in a marina in Amble, a small seaport town midway between Newcastle and Lindisfarne.

I had good reason to be fretting over the anchor: the past few days sailing up the east coast from Lowestoft had proven some of the most challenging of the journey so far, and I wanted to make sure there was no chance of us being left untethered and adrift in the North Sea.

The 40-knot squall near Great Yarmouth was an ominous start for the first leg of the journey up to Grimsby. Both the boat and the weather appeared to be conspiring against me. First, the boat's fuel gauge stopped working. To reach my next scheduled stop in Grimsby, I would need to make sure I had enough fuel to be able to sail at night up the Humber, another of England's powerful tidal estuaries like the Thames.

This meant using the motor as little as possible and sailing whenever I could. However, the weather wasn't playing ball. For my whole journey up the East Anglia coast, the wind was blowing against me. Sailing into the wind isn't impossible – it is just painfully slow. It requires sailing 'close hauled', where you position the sails tight in, steering 40 degrees to the wind. It worked, but it meant that much of East Anglia's coast – lovely as it is – excruciatingly passed by me at walking pace. By the time I reached the top of the region and turned portside towards the Wash, a light headwind had picked up. Sailing close hauled would leave me stationary, so I had no choice but to fire up the motor and gently run the boat for six hours, using as little fuel as possible. Up until this point, I had yet again been failing to learn the recurring lesson of this mission: to lean into the Lord and rely on His provision. Instead, I had been relying purely on my sailing knowledge and expertise. After many hours of slowly watching Norfolk's sandy beaches give way to the salt marshes of the Wash, inching towards Lincolnshire, the penny finally dropped; I decided to pray about it. I prayed for wind – the right kind of wind – and God answered. A wind blew up from the south that enabled me to rig the spinnaker and travel a still relatively ponderous but very relaxing seven knots for the next eight hours, all the way to the entrance of the Humber.

This was my cue to fire up the motor once again and use the precious fuel to take me up the estuary. After 21 hours and 120 miles – averaging somewhere between 5 and 6 miles per hour - I finally arrived at the Humber Cruising Association marina in Grimsby Fish Docks at 1am. I have fond memories of this part of the world: my first job as a civil engineer was near Immingham, working on the construction of the M180 motorway while living with Deirdre as newlyweds in a caravan behind a pub in Brigg. I loved the place even more as I wearily walked up the gangway in the early hours of the morning to be greeted with a pint of beer handed to me by late-night revellers at the marina club house.

I had planned to take a rest day in Grimsby, but the snail's pace of my journey up from Lowestoft meant I was now a day behind from where I had planned to be. To keep to my schedule, I left at 9am that same morning, after refuelling, just hours after arriving. Leaving early was necessary to catch the tide that would take me out of the Humber estuary and back into the North Sea as I sailed 75 miles up to Scarborough for my next overnight stop, and then on another 85 miles to Newcastle in time for the Celebrate Northeast gathering the next evening.

Appropriately for this mission, the gathering took place at St. Peter's Marina, located on the north bank of the Tyne between the Byker and St. Anthony's neighbourhoods of Newcastle. Unfortunately, my tight schedule after the long haul up to Grimsby meant I had little time to venture far from the boat to enjoy the delights of this great city. Instead, after an evening's celebration with members of the Celebrate family from all over northeast England, I was setting sail again the next morning.

However, for the first time in a week I was not doing so alone: Julia Kelly, an active member of Celebrate North East, joined me for the relatively short 30-mile trip up to the Northumberland fishing town of Amble. It was a symbolic journey for Julia, representing her local Celebrate team taking the prayer mission out of Newcastle and sending me on my way to Holy Island. Julia prayed relentlessly as we sailed down the Tyne, interceding first for Newcastle and then her hometown, South Shields, as we passed it at the mouth of the river and returned to the North Sea. We headed north into Whitley Bay and up along the picturesque Northumberland coast, passing seals and puffins basking in the afternoon sun on Coquet Island as we reached our destination of Amble. Julia was having a tough time at work, and the trip amongst all this natural beauty was a moment of calm and a time to think and discern the direction of her career and life. It once again reminded me how the sea is a good place to be with God, to listen and reflect.

Amble marina was situated in the most stunning location of any so far on the journey: in a natural harbour where the River Coquet meets the North Sea. Sitting alongside an historic fishing village, the marina is surrounded by sand dunes and castles in Northumberland's Area of Outstanding Natural Beauty.

Julia had to get back soon after arriving in Amble and so I found myself alone on the boat that afternoon, practicing the anchor operation before my next crew member, John Wormall, joined me the following morning for the journey up to Lindisfarne.

Anchors on most boats are operated using a piece of equipment called a windlass. It is a mechanical winch with a clutch that allows you to wind out the chain so that the anchor hits the seabed in a controlled manner. It can also be easily wound back up when you want to set sail again.

The one thing you don't want to do with a windlass is have the anchor fall rapidly down to the bottom, with all the chain paying out and just dumping down with the anchor on the seabed. If you do this, the anchor won't work properly: you need to let out just enough chain and rope - collectively known as the rode - so that the anchor touches the bottom, then let the boat drift, let out a little more of the rode to allow the right balance between keeping the anchor and chain set on the seabed and the boat falling into a safe position.

It was a beautiful, calm and sunny afternoon in Amble. Feeling very relaxed and confident that this would be a routine test of the windlass and anchor, I started to let the chain out. To my horror, I had got the clutch wrong and all the chain just ran straight out of the boat, with the anchor and rode plummeting to the bottom of the river. Thankfully it was still tied to the boat, but I was left feeling unconfident and unprepared, thinking 'this blooming thing isn't going to work properly, and I've got John arriving tomorrow and we need to anchor off the Farne Islands and Holy Island'.

And then the Lord just gave me this image of what it was like for Christ, taking the consequence of our sin on Himself when

He was crucified. We sinned against the Lord, but not only was He prepared to forgive us for that, He was going to take the consequence of that sin - which we would otherwise have had to deal with - and put it on to himself. And what happened to Him on that cross - what the Lord was showing me - was that Christ, like the anchor, at the moment of His death was free-falling into hell. Carrying all that consequence of sin, Christ was totally divorced, separated from God. He was holding onto the end of the rope - his connection with the Father - and no matter how much He tried to pull on it, the rope just kept on paying out and Christ dropped into hell.

Sat there on the boat, staring into the murky water, searching for an anchor I couldn't see, the Lord showed me both that Christ is the anchor of our lives, and the horror that He endured for us, losing that feeling of security that He had always known: his connection with the Father. It was why, in that moment of horror, Jesus uttered the word on the cross 'Eli, Eli Lama Sabachthani', which is Aramaic for 'My God, my God, why have you forsaken me?'.

These words are also the opening of Psalm 22, written by David almost 1,000 years before Jesus was born, when enemies surrounded him. Jesus would have known these words well. He would also have known, even in His moment of despair, that in this Psalm David goes on to praise the Lord. David writes:

'He has not despised or scorned the suffering of the afflicted one; He has not hidden his face from him but has listened to his cry for help.' (Psalm 22:24)

Christ was and is always firmly tied to God the Father. He was tied to the Father during his time as Jesus here with us on Earth. He remained tied even when he was free-falling down and that connection to the Father, like the anchor's chain and rope, was paying out unchecked but still connected. And then at some point the Father, in His love and His mercy, allowed that connection, that line between Him and Christ, to bite. Slowly but surely, the Father pulled Christ out of Hell and back towards Him, raising Christ from the dead.

This image from the Lord also moved me from despair to hope. I worked out what I had done wrong with the clutch, and slowly but surely, bit by bit, I wound the anchor up from the river bed and back on to the boat with me. Confident I now knew how to operate the windlass, I was once again able to look forward to visiting some of the most beautiful, historic and holy places in Britain with a friend.

John Wormall is an old rugby buddy and drinking pal who I'd not seen for 25 years. He and his wife Sally had children before us and were inspirational in how to raise a family and still make the time to care for others... incredible people. I could not contain my excitement at seeing him again, a man full of life and fun to be around. He is not someone who would describe himself as a Christian, but he is a good-hearted pragmatic adventurer who I thought would be up to the challenge of this leg of the voyage, exposed to wind and waves from across the North Sea, with few safe harbours to shelter in. He would go on to call the three days we spent together an experience he would never forget. I believe the special experience John had, came from a combination of being in the boundless beauty of creation, the almost tangible presence of peace and holiness that can be found on the Farne Islands and Lindisfarne, and witnessing the change in me, his old friend, as every day I learnt more about how to step out in faith. That, and the excitement of flying along for several days under spinnaker in winds approaching 20 knots, and spending the nights at anchor, lying tight up to rocky shores.

John's sense of humour, courage and sense of adventure shone through, and brought back fond memories of our younger days. There's a line in Matthew's Gospel that simply says, 'Jesus went for a walk in the cornfield on the Sabbath'. That's it. There's no purpose to Jesus' walk that we are told of, although he goes on to deliver a lesson on the Sabbath after his disciples pluck the corn and eat it, provoking anger among the Pharisees. But the original reason for the walk is never explained. He just went for a walk in a cornfield. What I think the Lord was doing with this mission, apart from all the prayer, was that he just wanted to go for a walk in a cornfield with us. The wonder of creation draws a lot of people to Him and he has created it for us to enjoy it. There are few, if any places, better to enjoy it in the UK than in the Farne Islands.

We left Amble and spent the day sailing up the Northumbrian coast. Our first stop, and our first anchorage, was in a small body of water known as The Kettle, in the Inner Farne Islands. Being able to anchor here made all my earlier trials with the anchor

worthwhile: Sir David Attenborough has called the Farne
Islands his favourite place in the UK to see 'magnificent nature',
and it was easy to see why.

As well as grey seals playing in the water and lounging
on the rocky edges of the islands, there were what seemed
like countless numbers of different species there. This is
unsurprising when you consider that over 100,000 seabirds
visit the Farne Islands every year. At the time of year that John
and I were there – mid-May – the islands and waters around
them play host to puffins, eider ducks, kittiwakes, fulmars,
guillemots, razorbills, sandwich terns, common terns, shags, and
Arctic terns, among others. We were there at the perfect time to
see the Arctic terns: they arrive in early May, but towards the
end of the month their young are hatching and the terns start
dive-bombing sailors and anyone who comes too close to their
nesting brood.

The eider ducks are also nesting during May, and it is this
species that ties together the Farne Islands and the Holy Island
of Lindisfarne to their north. The Farne Islands have the oldest
wildlife protection laws of anywhere on the planet, enacted by
St. Cuthbert in 676 A.D. Cuthbert was prior of the monastery at
Lindisfarne, and in 675 he visited the Farnes for a period of
solitude and reflection. He became interested in the seabirds on
the islands and discovered that local people liked to eat the eider
ducks and their eggs. As a result, he introduced the world's first
bird protection laws to protect the eider ducks and other
seabirds nesting on the islands.

Cuthbert loved the Farne Islands so much that he retired as prior of Lindisfarne Monastery and lived on Inner Farne as a hermit, before being persuaded to come out of retirement eight years later to become Bishop of Lindisfarne for the last three years of his life. He is the patron saint of Northumberland, and as we left the Farne Islands to spend time at Lindisfarne, visiting its Castle and the ruins of the monastery, it seemed highly appropriate to be following in St. Cuthbert's footsteps: Lindisfarne, established as a monastery by St. Aidan from the Celtic Iona community in Scotland, was the base from which Celtic Christian monks evangelised Northern England and Southern Scotland.

Born in Dunbar, Scotland, in 634 A.D., Cuthbert is understood to have had a vision to become a monk on the same night St. Aidan died in 651 A.D. and joined Melrose Abbey in the Scottish borders. He joined Lindisfarne as prior four years later, embarking on missionary work that stretched from his base on the east coast all the way to Galloway in south-western Scotland, and as far north as Berwick.

Not only was Cuthbert a great missionary for me to take inspiration from on this trip, but he was also – again particularly appropriate for our mission – a unifying figure for a divided country. After his death on Inner Farne in 687 A.D., Alfred the Great, King of Wessex, had a dream where Cuthbert inspired him in his struggles against the Danes. After this the Royal House of Wessex, who became the kings of England, had a devotion to St. Cuthbert. This devotion to a saint from the northeast by a royal house from the far south of the country helped unite the many different counties and kingdoms as one England.

John and I had a few wonderful days exploring the beauty of these historic islands. We would visit sites such as Lindisfarne monastery, where I found time to pray and John would stand back and take it all in. Each evening we rowed our little dinghy back to the anchored boat, where we cooked dinner, and thanked God for his creation and for looking after us. Our experiences on the Farne Islands and Lindisfarne would be the first of many on this mission to develop in me a great sense of the pioneering work that Christians did in the early times, setting up missions in caves on islands, being the lonely voices in the wilderness evangelising the nation. I felt very affirmed here in the calling to be a pioneer in these modern times and be a voice in what does at times seem like a wilderness; in all the places where I live, work, play and rest. It may seem difficult at times, but it's what I've signed up for in my baptism and confirmation.

As we sailed out of Lindisfarne, three huge dolphins appeared and stayed with the boat to escort us around the headland - a great send-off for the next leg to Eyemouth on the southern Scottish coast. I nicknamed these escorts Father, Son and Holy Spirit, and it was a fitting end to a peaceful few days spent basking in the awesome splendour of God's great creation, and the peaceful serenity of this holy site. What followed next was anything but serene: John and I had a thrilling surf of a sail under spinnaker to Eyemouth, only to spend a boisterous night at anchor, followed by a cold and windy 60-mile reach across a murky Firth of Forth. It was tough stuff for two old muckers like John and me, but we loved every minute of it.

CREW TESTIMONY
JOHN WORMALL

My fondest memory of the mission was waking up in the harbour on the second day to see a fantastic sunrise, seemingly coming up alone, shining on nothing but our boat and the sea. The second fondest memory was going on to Holy Island, which was beautiful and emotional. It was me and Russ - my old school friend - living the dream.

I jumped at the chance to join the mission when Russ asked me. I have zero faith, but I thought it would be a great experience to do it with my old mate who I had played Rugby with, and who I had been in boats with before during our school days.

The one thing about Russ's faith was it was infectious. If I was going to find faith it would be on the boat in interesting weather. Our arrival into Arbroath harbour, where we were tossed about even when we reached the mooring, was a time when I saw a side of Russ I knew I had not got. Russ was so cool and we needed some help from someone, maybe God! I thought I would have been praying in those conditions, but at the time I decided I would leave that to Russ. I knew that if we got into trouble Russ could have faith for both of us. In the end, we needed each other and faith, I think. And I'd happily do it all again!

Praying the mission scroll in Newcastle

The Holy Island of Lindisfarne from the boat and on foot with John

SIX

FRIENDS IN HIGH PLACES
(ARBROATH TO OBAN)

'What a day that would be, when the beauty of the sea,
the mountains, a bird, overwhelms me.
What a day that would be…
when I am so overwhelmed in the joy of
loving a new friend and introducing
them to my dearest friend, no matter the cost.
What a day that would be.'
(Russ Fairman)

BATMAN HAD ROBIN, FRODO HAD SAMWISE, MOSES HAD AARON, and Paul had Barnabas and Timothy. Friends are an essential part of any adventure story, and this pilgrimage was no different. Going on an adventure never means doing so alone. You always need the help and companionship of friends. Even Jesus Christ, God incarnate, chose to carry out his three years of earthly ministry in the company of his twelve apostles.

For me, although there were times when I sailed solo, I was never on my own: before I set sail I had enlisted a small army of prayer warriors to intercede daily for me and the mission. And on the boat itself, this journey was one where new friendships were being formed constantly, and some old ones were being deepened: John and I parted company in Arbroath, each of us saying farewell to a much closer friend than the old rugby drinking buddy we had greeted three days earlier.

Our watery pilgrimage was now firmly in Scotland, slightly ahead of schedule, and I was excited to meet the next crew, who kindly switched their pick-up point to this beautiful picture postcard harbour at Arbroath. This vibrant fishing town with its houses painted in varying vivid greens, yellows and pinks, is famous for the 'Arbroath Smokie ' - a form of smoked haddock - but the most visible signs of fishing in the marina came from another local seafood delicacy: stacked high all along one end of the harbor wall were masses of lobster pots.

My two new crewmates and soon-to-be friends were husband and wife Ann and Robert Kerr. We spent the afternoon and evening getting acquainted with an on-board meal and prayer time, which by now had become my regular crew-change routine. I must mention the fantastic welcome we received from parishioners after Mass at the local Catholic church, St. Thomas of Canterbury Arbroath. This parish community lavished us with tea and cake, introducing themselves as we sat together chatting in the church hall. They went out of their way to tell us how wonderful the new Polish parishioners were in supporting the church; we later found out they were not so well received by all sections of the community in the town, due to job shortages. We prayed with them for the economic wellbeing of Arbroath, thanking God for the welcome of strangers and for the blessing that the Polish community was in the town. Neither Robert nor Ann had attended a Celebrate event before, but they were regular church-goers and occasional sailors, and a friend had recommended they get in touch. As it turned out, it was a real blessing to have fellow sailors onboard with me for this next leg, which was to be far more challenging than I could have anticipated.

I had arrived in Arbroath on Saturday 18th May – day 21 of the mission – and I set sail with the Kerrs on the Sunday morning after Mass. Ann and Robert were sailing with me for four days, from Arbroath to Inverness. These would be four days of long distances and a significant milestone for the pilgrimage: this leg would mark the point where we would 'turn the corner ' and stop heading north, instead moving west and then south towards the start of the Caledonian Canal.

I had planned for our first stop on this leg to be Peterhead, another major fishing town with a large bay protected by breakwaters. Situated on the eastern tip of Scotland, Peterhead is 30 miles north of Aberdeen and just under 80 miles north of Arbroath. It was the perfect location for an overnight stop after putting in some decent miles in the wilds of the North Sea. The Lord, and the weather, had other plans: between Aberdeen and Peterhead thick fog descended. Unable to see further than two boat lengths, we pressed on slowly, trusting in the AIS vessel tracking system (while wishing I also had radar, as fishing boats notoriously turn off their AIS as they track fish shoals), and kept alert to any sounds or shapes in the thick fog. We did so carefully, gingerly inching through the water at walking pace. By the time we were approaching Peterhead it was 4am on Monday morning, and the fog was still covering us on every side. I decided it was preferable to press on, rather than attempt heading into the port. We 'turned the corner ' of Scotland and as we started heading west along Aberdeenshire's northern coast, the fog finally began to lift - thank God. I now needed to consult the chart and find the nearest safe place to stop.

After 110 miles of sailing day and night, we finally arrived in the small fishing village of Whitehills on Monday morning. It was an old fishing quay, just the type of rough-walled structure where I thought I may need the fender board to help us safely moor up. Thankful to be out of the fog and having a rest thanks to an old piece of junk wood, I decided to see if there might be some Celebrate connection to this place that we had unexpectedly landed in. I rang Ged Farrell, the man at the heart of Celebrate Scotland, a gentle giant so well connected that if anybody was going to know somebody here, Ged would. Unbeknown to me he lived just 20 miles inland from Whitehills and met us for lunch onboard with his lovely wife Margaret.

After lunch, Ged said: 'This has been such a lovely encounter with you guys. I'm going to call the people in our charismatic prayer group from the northeast of Scotland, who are meeting this evening and see if they wouldn't mind travelling over here.' And they did! It meant that, after meeting friends across the country in large towns and cities, we now had our fifth Celebrate gathering in Whitehills, a fishing village with the population of a mid-sized secondary school. This spontaneous moment of praise and worship on the quayside with guitars strumming was joyous, and like so much of this leg of the trip had a powerful effect on Ann and Robert, really cementing their newfound relationship with the Celebrate family and drawing them deeper into their faith.

After the lavish reception from parishioners in Arbroath, and the wonderful impromptu gathering in Whitehills, it was dawning on me that what I was experiencing in this part of Scotland was something special: the generosity, the hospitality and the warmth of the people were charming me, but also continuing to build my faith. Just as the Lord greeted us in prayer on the boat, he was surrounding us with the goodness of people when we stepped onshore.

At Lossiemouth, our next stop along the almost tropical sandy beach and pine forest-encrusted northern coast, the harbour-master spotted the boat's flags as we entered the marina. When I went up to her office to pay the marina fee, she asked: 'I noticed the flags on your boat, are you some kind of Christian charity?' It's the sort of question that prior to the pilgrimage I had been apprehensive about. You never quite know how these things will be received. You don't know if it's going to upset people or if they're going to react in a negative way. I told her that we were on a sailing mission praying with people and raising money for a youth programme called Joel's Bar.

True to form for this part of Scotland, instead of any kind of negative reaction, the harbourmaster beamed as she said: 'Well you're not paying anything for staying here tonight. I'm waiving the marina fee.' She then pulled out a Scottish £20 note and pressed it into my hand, saying that it was for Joel's Bar. I thanked her profusely, offered to pray for her, and returned to Ann and Robert on the boat to relay the good news. We felt so secure in this incredibly beautiful little harbour, lounging in the cockpit all afternoon in the warm sunshine, sharing our lives' stories. While Robert slept below, Ann went deeply into an area of pain for her: the loss of her heroic brother, who stepped in to avert a domestic affray was later murdered in retaliation. Ann is an amazing woman of faith, with an infectious enthusiasm for life, and taught me a lot about forgiveness and the mixed emotions that surround a tragedy - only God has the power to really heal such wounds and restore us to be fully alive.

From Lossiemouth we sailed into the Moray Firth under the watchful eye of the imposing Morven mountain in Caithness. We were escorted by dolphins as we sailed at an exhilarating pace of 9 knots towards the Kerrs' destination of Inverness. As I said goodbye to two new friends who had found their faith deepened during their time on the boat, I prepared to greet two old friends the next day, both enlisted to help me navigate the Caledonian Canal while passing through some of the most beautiful scenery in the UK.

Engineers first started considering connecting the Moray Firth with Fort William, 60 miles southwest of Inverness, in the early 1700s. Even though it would have been a herculean task to build it back then, it's easy to see why they wanted to try: it would boost Scottish trade by providing a link between Scotland's east and west coasts, and it would remove the need for sailors like myself to circumnavigate the far north of Scotland and its treacherous seas. The canal was such a massive undertaking that it was nearly another hundred years before work would start in 1805, and a further 17 years until it was completed. Based on Scottish engineering icon Thomas Telford's plan to link Loch

Ness, Loch Oich and Loch Lochy, this waterway through the Great Glen was the biggest canal in the world when it was completed in 1822, requiring 22 miles of cuttings to link these spectacular Lochs.

Flowing through the Highlands and in the shadow of Ben Nevis, the canal also needed 28 locks to navigate the mountainous terrain. It was because of this that, when planning the trip, I knew I would need two fit and able crewmates to help take the ropes and get Mintaka through the canal's many locks.

Guy Martin and Glenn Gerrard were two former colleagues of mine who, like John Wormall, weren't practicing Christians - although Glenn has Catholic family roots and Guy sings in choral choirs - but they were up for having an adventure through some of Scotland's most majestic landscapes. What they hadn't bargained with was having to become spokesmen for the mission.

In late May, the canal is teeming with tourists and pleasure cruisers. At every lock, I would stay onboard to steer Mintaka through, while Guy and Glenn would jump up either side, holding the ropes to ensure the boat's plastic body didn't go crashing into the rough lock walls (thank you fender board). As anyone who has ever taken a canal holiday will know, going through a lock is anything but a fast experience. Guy and Glenn were therefore stood either side of the lock for long periods, with onlookers and passers-by asking them questions like 'What are these flags about? ' and 'What if it's true', so what does that mean?'. And they would have to stand there and explain all about Celebrate and the pilgrimage, and I would laugh and joke with them about becoming evangelists each time they climbed back onboard after a lock.

On the second of four days travelling down the canal, I had the opportunity to do another interview with BBC local radio about the mission. BBC Radio Solent presenter Tim Daykin first broadcast an interview between me and his reporter Sarah Bassett a couple of weeks before the mission started. He then sent Sarah along for our false-start send-off on Saturday 27th April and now, a month later – Sunday 26th May to be precise - he carried out a phone interview with me live from the Caledonian Canal.

There is a perception among many people I know – and in some cases it may be justified – that there is a media bias in the UK against Christians and Christianity. To what extent that is true I don't know, but I do know that when we as Christians find a friend in the media like Tim Daykin, we should support them, celebrate them, and pray for them. Not only did Tim check in regularly with us throughout the pilgrimage, but he also connected me to other local BBC radio programmes across the country that would interview me later in the mission.

The interview on the Caledonian Canal was fairly brief, just an update on how we were doing and some of the experiences so far. If Tim had called a few days later, I would have had some even more amazing tales for him.

Glenn, Guy and I reached Fort William on Tuesday 28th May, and we took the opportunity to spend the next couple of days enjoying the natural beauty of the Sound of Mull, with its castles, dolphins and exhilarating sailing, before heading to Oban to change crew. Our friendship was solid enough before, but this trip with all its laughter, joy, and excitement cemented something very special between us, that I will treasure forever - sailing has a habit of doing that.

Oban is a beautiful little town on Scotland's west coast. Named after the Gaelic word for 'little bay ', its picturesque surroundings of beaches, mountains and castles, and a ferry terminal offering day trips from here to islands such as Mull and Iona, mean its principal industry is tourism. Glenn, Guy and I arrived there on the Thursday after the second May Bank Holiday, during the school summer half term. It was bursting with tourists. We joined the throngs to wander around its various delights, including a couple of museums. Glenn and Guy were due to head off that afternoon, so we decided to grab a farewell lunch together before they departed.

It was at this point that I reached into my jacket pocket and grasped at the empty space where my wallet should have been. I had lost it! The wallet had nearly £300 in cash to cover marina fees, food and fuel during the pilgrimage, plus all my credit and bank cards. We retraced our steps but to no avail. I didn't want to hold up Glenn and Guy any further, so we had lunch and they paid. They also gave me what little cash they had in their wallets to tide me over.

We embraced each other, and once again I said goodbye to closer friends than I had at the start of this trip. Then I was alone, in a remote part of the Scottish mainland off the Inner Hebrides, praying that the Lord would once again deliver a miracle to keep me moving on this mission.

And my phone rang. It was Paul, an old school friend of mine who lived in Reading. We hadn't spoken for a long time, and he didn't know about the mission, but as I was praying for a miracle he had decided to give me a call. He was in Oban, completely unaware that I was there too. He explained that he had come for a diving trip around the islands with friends, and I told him how I was praying for a miracle and he might just be it. Paul is a successful businessman and when he heard my predicament he offered to loan me £1,000 in cash, which he came and delivered in person to me at the marina later that afternoon. This money would be enough to fund the trip as far as Liverpool when my son Sam would be joining me and could bring up newly issued bank cards from home.

The next morning, I sat on the deck of Mintaka having my breakfast, looking out at the water and the mountains overlooking Oban, and looking forward to the next leg of the mission with my new crewmate Martin, who was to join me in 24 hours' time. My phone rang again. It was the Oban Marina Office saying they had just had a call from an officer at Oban police station. My wallet, which contained a marina receipt, had been handed in. When I arrived at the Police station it was a wonderful affirmation of the kindness of strangers that I had encountered so far in Scotland: the wallet was full, with every single pound of cash and every card inside.

The Lord was blessing me through both the kindness of strangers and deepening of friendships on this pilgrimage. He was also deepening his relationship with me and was about to do it in a profound way with the arrival of my next crewmate and our journey through the Inner and Outer Hebrides.

Impromptu praise and worship in the Scottish village of Whitehills

On the Caledonian Canal going past Ben Nevis

PART TWO

THE WEST COAST

SEVEN

THE LORD GETS IN THE BOAT
(OBAN & INNER HEBRIDES)

'Therefore, if anyone is in Christ, the new creation has come:
The old has gone, the new is here!'
(St. Paul's Second Letter to the Corinthians,
Chapter 5 Verse 17)

OF ALL MY CREWMATES ON THE MISSION, FEW LEFT A GREATER impression on me than Martin. He's a man-mountain and I easily recognised him as he made his way towards me in Oban Marina the day after I had been reunited with my wallet.

Martin had described himself as 'big ' during a phone call several months earlier, when he did his best to dissuade me from having him onboard as crew. He called me from his home in Scotland, his heavy Mancunian accent betraying his roots.

'I've got your number from a friend in the Charismatic Renewal who saw an advert for your trip,' he began. 'I've got a prayer life, and I'd like to come with you. I've got a heart for praying for the country, a love of the sea although I've never been on a sailboat before. But I've done some terrible things in my life. and I don't deserve to come. If anybody else comes to you after me and would like to go, then I'll just back out.'

I replied: 'Martin, we're all broken men. You have every right to come on this mission and I want you on the mission even more now you've said this. '

'But you need to know that I was a criminal, a serious criminal. And I've been in most of the prisons in northern England.'

Martin told me his story; of how he once worked in Manchester for the family gangs who ran the doors of the night clubs and controlled much of the city's drug dealing. Like most, he had started from an early age. His substantial size and reputation for being a good scrapper at school soon led the gangs to groom him, showering him with gold jewellery, girls, and BMWs.

They made him a king, and in return Martin's job was to collect the drug money from the dealers. In doing so, he assaulted and seriously hurt many people, had been in and out of prison many times, and had even escaped once. It was during his final stretch in prison that Martin came to the Lord. It was a massive conversion for a massive man, centred on a very Catholic devotion to the Rosary and a little prayer book called The Pieta, a collection of Catholic prayers and devotions. He has since built a new life for himself and his family in Scotland.

After telling me all of this over the phone, he then said: 'There's something else that might be a bit of an issue...' I was silently thinking what else could there possibly be? 'I'm 20-odd stone.' Now this bothered me far more than Martin's past, as the sleeping bunks on the boat were narrow and there wasn't a huge amount of room below deck in the cockpit. Martin could hear my hesitation down the line and quickly followed up 'I'm not fat... just big! '

Martin was therefore easy to spot as he walked towards me along the marina's gangway, towering above us sailors down on the water. I had already explained to Martin over the phone that we would have a few days to pass in and around Oban before a couple more crewmates would join us for the onward journey to Glasgow.

He stood by the boat, rosary beads the size of marbles hanging from his neck, anchored by a huge cross resting on his chest. This was clearly a man on fire for the Lord. 'So, what are we going to do then? ' he asked.

I explained that I had already been praying with people in Oban. 'Great, let's do that '

I may have prayed with a few strangers in the town, but I did it in my very relaxed and casual manner. Martin, on the other hand, really was a man on a mission.

As we walked along towards the ferry terminal – a place I knew would be bustling – he prayed the Rosary continuously. Even before we reached the ferry terminal, Martin was stopping people, joking and having a laugh with them, then sharing his story. And they couldn't really say no to a man like Martin. Once we were at the ferry terminal he was off, in among the throng praying with whoever he could. I caught up with him just as he met a couple – James and Elli - who were there to celebrate their wedding anniversary. We offered a small prayer of thanksgiving and then, sensing there was more, we pressed further, asked if there was anything else. Small tears began forming in Elli's eyes as she explained they had only one child, Sarah, who was now a young woman and wanted to go to India volunteering.

'I don't want to let her go,' said Elli. 'I know she's old enough to do it, but I'm frightened that I might lose her. She's the only child I could have… she's incredibly precious.'

We prayed for her anxiety over this situation, and for Sarah's safety. We could immediately see Elli's body softening as we prayed, becoming less tense, and she told us she felt a greater sense of peace over the situation. They both thanked us and made their way to their ferry.

Just as Veronica Langford's unabashed enthusiasm had rubbed off on me all those weeks ago in London, so too I found spending time in Martin's company made me more keenly aware of the Lord's presence, and more desperate to share the Good News with others.

After a full day of praying around Oban, I went to the shop to buy food and drink for the next few days. I can only say I was glad Deirdre wasn't with me – she is a street evangelist herself, but being a proficient shopper for our big family, would have lost patience as I offered prayer to anyone the Lord prompted me to engage with, and they seemed to come along like London buses, with prayer continuing all the way up to the cashier.

Despite this lengthy prayer walk for groceries, Martin insisted that he wanted to treat me to a local fish meal cooked on board. I didn't fancy our chances of finding anything open this late on a Saturday in Oban. But Martin was insistent.

We set off from the marina and strode into town towards the fishmongers. Sure enough, it was closed. But there was an alleyway to the side of the shop and the noise of someone busily moving around towards the back of the building.

'Let's take a look, ' said Martin, with a wink. After a bit of enthusiastic knocking, a rosy cheeked fishmonger sheepishly opened the door, with a less than welcoming greeting. We explained who we were and what we were doing both generally with the mission, and more specifically what we were doing in the back of her shop late on a Saturday afternoon. After a bit of banter, she told us her name was Carol and to my surprise she accepted our offer of prayer. At her request we prayed for her business, her family, her happiness. To my further surprise Carol then opened the cold room and sold us the fish and scallops Martin had asked for... mission accomplished in every respect. What a banquet we had that night. As well as being a fantastic prayer warrior to have alongside me on this mission, Martin also happened to be a great cook: no shop sauces for him, everything cooked from scratch: 'reduce, reduce, reduce' was his catch-phrase. His proficiency in the kitchen was a revelation and blessing to me – my cooking skills are somewhat limited and the five set recipes Deirdre taught me to see me through the pilgrimage were starting to get a bit repetitive after five weeks at sea.

The morning after our banquet was a sailor's dream, with a moderate breeze bathed in sunshine. I had planned for us to sail out of Oban and follow the ferry route up the Sound of Mull to the picturesque town of Tobermory – made famous by the children's TV programme Balamory – where we would spend the night. Not only is this town a beautiful spot, but I also knew that Paul would be there, and I wanted to acknowledge his incredible kindness and generosity to me in Oban. We were best pals at school and my wife Deirdre had exchanged Christmas cards every year with Paul and his wife, which had kept the link for a re-connection 25 years later. There's something about obedience and faithfulness that I have a lot to learn. And, of course, it was a chance to bring the prayer ministry that we had delivered in Oban to the Isle of Mull.

We sailed up the Sound of Mull in clear open water, looking towards snow-capped mountains on the distant horizon, singing and praying as we went. We sang songs of worship, we prayed for the people we had met in Oban, and we prayed for those that we were going to meet in Tobermory. As we did, a deep grace came upon us: we both became silent, feeling the unmistakable peace and bliss that comes with the presence of the Holy Spirit. It didn't last for very long, but it was a special moment.

Tobermory soon came into view – it is just 27 miles north of Oban, taking us just over an hour to sail – and Martin was getting excited. I, on the other hand, was slowing the boat down.

'Come on then, are we going in?' asked Martin.

'No,' I replied. Despite sorely wanting to go in and meet up with Paul, I had the sense that the Lord was saying something. That ability to hear him, which I had long prayed for, seemed to be kicking in.

'Come on, it looks beautiful,' insisted Martin. 'No Martin. I think the Lord is saying we need to hold off and pray.'

We stopped by a waterfall at a cliff outside the bay, we looked towards Tobermory, and we prayed. Once again that deep grace came upon us, but even more powerfully and for longer. This time we weren't silent. I was no longer conscious of my own words as the Holy Spirit guided my prayer. We went deep into prayer for Tobermory, Mull and Scotland. It was amazing.

And then, as the grace lifted and we both recovered our self-awareness, Martin said: 'This has been wonderful. I can't wait to get into Tobermory and go into one of those quaint-looking pubs... it looks so pretty!' 'I'm sorry Martin, but the Lord is still saying no.'

The further I went in this pilgrimage, the easier it was becoming to discern promptings from Holy Spirit. This direction about Tobermory in particular was very clear to me - a spiritual communication with vivid clarity and assuredness of origin. So, although I didn't know why I was being directed in this way, I just said: 'We're going to sail out and anchor overnight on the other side of the Sound.'

'But we're here now. We came all this way to go to Tobermory.'

Despite Martin's protestations, I told him we would instead be going to an isolated cove on what looked like an island in the Sound. The 'island' I was referring to was Oronsay, a tidal island that is actually more of a peninsula. There's a crack in the rock on this peninsula that is large enough to sail through, and it opens into a cove called Loch na Droma Buidhe.

We sailed in through the rock to balmy calm stillness. 'Ah Russ, what a great call. This looks amazing.'

I thought, 'no Martin, this looks a bad call, a very bad call indeed'. If you have ever been to Scotland in balmy calm, it's both pretty and terrible: midges are everywhere and they have the nasty habit of descending and covering you in bites.

I could see all around the loch were clouds of midges. Perhaps I didn't have a newfound ability for hearing the Lord after all – or if I did something had definitely been lost in translation.

'We're not going to stay here Martin, ' I said. 'We'll get eaten alive unless we lock everything down and tape up the gaps to stop them coming into the cabin.'

It was Martin's turn to be the one trusting the Lord with our movement: 'Well, let's just pray first.'

We got in the cockpit and we started to pray. Strangely, the midges didn't descend into the boat. Martin smiled at me, but with a nervous laugh I blurted out: 'Seriously… forget cooking dinner, we are going to be the evening meal if we stay here any longer.'

But even as I said it, I thought, 'Something's going on here. ' You don't just sit amongst a cloud of midges and not be lunch, dinner and tea all together.

We pressed on with our prayer. The grace that we had received in Tobermory came back on us. And then, all I can say is that the Lord got into the boat - physically got into the boat - with the two of us. He said: 'I love you boys. I love you. I love the friendship you formed. I love what you're doing. I love you.'

And then the sun, slowly setting, shone through the crack in the cove and lit up the cockpit. We'd stopped praying by that point as we just couldn't speak.

The sun passed, the light that had flooded the cockpit ebbed away and we came to our senses. We looked at each other and just cried.

Like so many other profound experiences on this mission, I don't think it was really for me. I was just a happy bystander, a witness to the Lord's work. No, that was all for Martin. It was the Lord confirming to him that there was an old Martin, but he has gone and there's a new Martin. The Lord was saying, 'Don't listen to the lies, you're completely worthy of a life with me. '

CREW TESTIMONY
MARTIN GREENHALGH

'If I say 'I will not mention him, or speak in his name,
then within me is something like a burning fire
shut up in my bones. I am weary with
holding it in, and I cannot.'
(Jeremiah chapter 20 verse 9)

Did I sign up for the mission or was I signed up by the Father? I love being near water because I am at peace there - even if I am not so confident in it - and I kept reading the Facebook posts of Russ' mission page. I saw his call to fill a few empty spaces that were left...or were they divinely reserved? I spoke to Russ and let him know that I could come aboard on the legs where he had a vacant space - where and when wasn't an issue for me.

This led to so many wonderful and profound spiritual moments during my time on board. I have left the retelling of our meeting with the Father at Loch na Droma Buidhe to Russ.

But another profound moment I would like to share was near the finale of my time on the boat: I had a powerful moment of grace where the sun shone on me through a cloudy, stormy sky. The grace said to me: 'I am the light of life, and darkness shall never overcome me. Those who accept the light of life shall have eternal life!' There is no doubt in my mind this was Jesus.

There were also physical graces every day we sailed. One day dolphins were racing alongside the boat matching its many knots of speed, then dipping out and in of a still, mill pond-like sea when we had stopped. Another evening - the night Russ and I spent at Loch na Droma Buidhe - a tall galleon-like ship came to anchor adjacent to us, which after our experience that day felt like the Fathers' grace saying, 'I am with you always.' Likewise at —James Watt Marina when a big super yacht moored adjacent to us. 'I am always with you!' My faith grew in assuredness.

There were also some funny moments. Russ was desperate to buy flowers for an elderly lady who had found his lost wallet with the voyage money in it and handed it in to the police. We went shopping and found ourselves walking down a tired industrious back street of Oban. We stopped and Russ said, 'I need to find this florist for those flowers! 'You could tell it was weighing heavy on Russ' mind to say thank you to this lady. And as he said the words, we looked and realised we were standing next to the only florist in Oban. We both looked up to the sky and then smiled at each other. The Lord made sure we were well catered for on the mission.

There are so many, many, fond memories. The friendships made, the graces felt, the people we met and prayed with. So many, but you know when I lost sight of God in my previous years, I lost how to love too. When we docked at Glasgow on Pentecost, I remember my two young boys running down the gangway to greet me and I them: in all their life we had never spent so much time apart. Jesus made me feel exactly how he must have felt when I returned to him, and how this love felt.

Since the sailing mission, myself and my family have opened a Bistro called 'El.' El is one of Judaism's seven names for God, and the cafe is about getting the word of God out. We want to let people know that you can have a personal encounter with God. We have talked with and prayed over people there. In doing so we have hopefully guided the curious, the weak, the weary, those who have forgotten how to love and those who have forgotten God, to realise a new way back to him.

Due to COVID-19, we only traded for nine weeks before closing due to lockdown. While we were only open for a short period of time, our remit had been filled - to get the word of the Lord out to people - it was never about earning money. That was secondary in nature. As a family in Christ, we are just waiting for the next opportunity to get the word out by God's grace. I think St Teresa of Calcutta said once: 'We ourselves feel that what we are doing is just a drop in the ocean. But the ocean would be less because of that missing drop.'

I would join Russ for a mission on the ocean again in a heartbeat, at the start of a pistol, by the signing up of my Father. If anyone gets the chance to do this kind of mission, my advice is don't miss it. This changes your life for the richer. To know the Father is to be rich beyond your wildest dreams.

Martin below deck doing two of his favorite things:
praying and cooking

Basking in the beauty of God's creation at Loch Linnhe

EIGHT

HILL OF FIRE
(OBAN TO GLASGOW)

'Praise be to the God and Father of our Lord Jesus Christ,
the Father of compassion and the God of all comfort,
who comforts us in all our troubles,
so that we can comfort those in any trouble
with the comfort we ourselves receive from God.'
(St. Paul's second letter to the Corinthians,
chapter 1 verses 3-4)

THERE IS SOMETHING ABOUT SAILING INTO A PLACE THAT IS profoundly spiritual. Coming in from the sea gives you a unique perspective and understanding of the natural context for a port or harbour. God's creation turns into a man's creation, and you get a sense of economic vibrancy from a city's docks, its fishing port, and you start homing in on it as a community.

It is a perspective that you rarely glimpse when driving into a town. You just don't get the same historical essence of the place when arriving by car, you don't get the fact that it's centred in something beautiful, created by God. Approaching every place we visited by sea really added greater depth to our intercessory prayers for the health of the nation, and particularly for those ports that we were sailing into at that time.

One such place was the beautiful loch-side beach of Ardentinny, steeped in ancient invasion and settlement history due to its ability to land a whole fleet of ships there. We were visiting Ardentinny while sailing from Oban to Glasgow for the next Celebrate gathering, at the special request of one of our new crew members, John Bain, born and bred in Glasgow. He and Matt Tozer had joined Martin and me at Oban, two days after our extraordinary experience at Loch na Droma Buide.

We spent the night anchored in the Loch, basking in the Holy Spirit, then returned to Oban early the next morning to moor up in the marina before a storm swept in that would keep us confined to the town for the rest of the day. Martin and I used this opportunity to spend our final day on our own to minister to the town's inhabitants and visitors one last time.

Our two new shipmates were also men who loved the Lord and were coming to the boat with their own stories filled with joy and pain. Matt Tozer is a young lad with a brain tumour, but he does not let his condition define who he is. Instead, he throws himself wholeheartedly into life, signing up for crazy things such as this mission, and has found a grace to be able to thank God for his tumour, insofar as it has made him who is.

John Bain, meanwhile, is a musician whose past, like Martin's, had much darkness in it. His father was an alcoholic. John would take him food every day, and every day his father would greet him with, 'Where's my drink?!' Each time John would tell his father that there was no alcohol, his father replying, 'I don't want your food, I want drink.' He would then verbally abuse

John, deriding his special needs and saying things such as 'you're a rubbish son', and 'your older brother was a better son to me ' before slamming the door. After a few moments the door would then reopen and John's father would quickly take in the food off the step and shut the door again. Through all this and other hardships, John has come to know the love of his real Father, who he trusts to never put him down, abuse him or reject him.

Week in, week out, for years and years, John would go back and take that abuse until his father passed away a few years ago. That kind of emotional abuse from a parent could crush a person. Instead, John moved his parenthood to the Lord, using his talents as a musician to praise his Father in Heaven daily.

John had brought his guitar with him, and so it was on a sunny balmy day that the four of us set sail out of Oban praising the Lord in song, while also navigating the rock-strewn Luing Sound and then gliding effortlessly past the beautiful islands of Lunga, Scarb and Jura.

With our big blue spinnaker aloft we headed on down the west coast of Kintyre, still praising our Lord through the Jura Sound, much to the bemusement of the seal colonies on the little islands that we passed. The Jura Sound is a place to bring you to your knees with its sheer beauty and the humbling power of its ferocious tidal races. I decided that we would spend the night anchored off the small Isle of Gigha, which sits adjacent to the Kintyre peninsula, looking out to Islay, world-famous for its smoky single-malt whisky. The sky was now ashen grey and a drizzle had set in with a building wind - hey it's Scotland after all - and we enjoyed being rocked to sleep at anchor, feeling smug that we'd sailed in sunshine and slept through the rain, stomachs full of another glorious dinner by Martin.

Gigha was the last safe spot in relatively calm waters before we would have to round the Mull of Kintyre. While it may have been popularised by Paul McCartney's sentimental and lilting song, for sailors the waters at the bottom of this peninsula are anything but gentle. Instead, they are notorious for races and steep waves as the Irish Sea crashes into the Firth of Clyde.

Having checked the tides and weather, we set sail at 6am to take advantage of the best of the day's sailing conditions. It was still a bumpy ride, but the rounding of the peninsular was far from the onslaught that it might otherwise have been... in fact the weather for the whole trip down from Oban was incredibly kind. We made it as far as the small town of Campbeltown, ten miles up the east coast of Kintyre, with its natural harbour and ferry crossings to both the Isle of Arran and mainland Scotland. Once again, we encountered fabulous Scottish generosity and hospitality as another harbour master refused to charge us for time spent in their marina, instead donating their fee to Joel's Bar.

We were in Campbeltown to pass the time before taking up another generous offer of hospitality that I had received while planning the mission. I was invited to sail the boat and its crew to Holy Isle, a small speck of an island off the east coast of the much larger Isle of Arran. The island has a long history as a sacred site, with a holy well spring with healing properties and a hermit cave once occupied in the 6th century by Irish monk Saint Molaise, which preceded a 13th-century monastery established on the island. Today the island is privately owned by Lama Yeshe Rinpoche, a Buddhist monk from Tibet. He has dedicated the island to spiritual purposes and established a Centre for World Peace and Health. In keeping with the island's heritage, the centre runs Christian and interfaith retreats in addition to Buddhist events, and Adam the centre's director invited us to come ashore and pray.

St. Molaise was born in Ireland, the son of Cairell, the Irish king of what is now called Ulster, and the Scottish princess Gemma. Molaise was a very gifted and spiritually inclined child. He was much loved by his own people and was offered the throne of Ulster when he came of age, but instead he chose a religious and secluded life in a cave on the west coast of Holy Isle. He was then only 20 years old. Some people believe that when St. Molaise chose the cave on Holy Isle as his hermitage, the island was already considered a special, 'holy' place.

When he was about 30 years old, Molaise went to Rome and was ordained as a priest by Pope Gregory the Great. When he returned, he entered the great monastery in Leighlin, Ireland. Soon after he became its abbot. Under his guidance the monastery grew in fame and number to about 1,500 monks.

We all felt the significance of this visit: Christians owe much to the faith of these early missionaries and it was moving to pray for Holy Isle, its inhabitants and visitors. I had a sense that St Molaise's faithful inspiration, and time spent in prayer away from worldly influence, is still required today to prepare us to seek a renewal and a turning back to God in our nation.

It was rather fitting that we were visiting a place dedicated to world peace, before heading on, as we were, to Ardentinny: a site linked with some of Scotland's bloodiest battles. Ardentinny lies just 30 miles north-northeast of Holy Isle as the crow flies. But in this majestic part of Scotland, the intricate network of headlands, islands and lochs means no journey on water – or land for that matter – can ever be as direct as the proverbial corvid bird.

It was enough just to get to our overnight stop in Tarbert on the shore of Loch Fyne. From our start in Campbeltown, over to Arran then Holy Isle, and up to Tarbert we ended up sailing 50 miles over the course of eight hours. And what a wonderful eight hours it was. We were treated to heavenly sailing, each of us dressed in shorts and T-shirts as the boat surfed along downwind in a force 6 all day in blazing sunshine.

At one point, coming the other way was a similar boat motoring with sails furled, seas breaking over the bow on every wave, and people dressed in oillies - heavy wet weather clothing - having a right old time of it. It made me think that my life can feel like this: hunkered down gritting my teeth into the wind, or going the other way sailing joyfully along with the wind, surrendered to the Lord. Being in the same place but going in a different direction is not really like being in the same place at all - the sea teaches you a lot.

We spent the night in the sensational harbour of Tarbert, a must visit place, by boat. In a bar that evening we met a local man called Don - a tough stoic character - who was fascinated by our mission but refused point blank our offer of prayer for himself. However, after a while he tearfully asked us to pray for his recently departed wife Gwen, who he missed dearly. So there and then we all held our hands over Don in his crowded local and prayed for Gwen. He then invited, no, insisted, we visit a park bench he had installed in honour of Gwen, on a hill overlooking Tarbert, giving us a picture of it he had in his wallet, and at the same time donating to Joel's Bar.

After this very moving encounter we were finally on our way to our ultimate destination of Glasgow and the next Celebrate Scotland gathering. More importantly for John, we would soon be making our stop at Ardentinny. Visiting this small hamlet on the coast of Loch Long was the main reason John was on this mission. Just as Veronica Langford's vision for London was a key reason for her taking part, when John signed up to crew the boat all those months ago, he made it very clear why he would be climbing aboard.

He had his own vision that we would sail to Ardentinny and pray for an end to generational violence in Scotland, and particularly in Glasgow, the city we would soon be heading to. Ardentinny's beach is the longest stretch of sand on the Cowal Peninsula, and this has made it a popular landing site for sailors of all kinds, from Gaelic raiders to British army commandos training during the Second World War, and tourists today. For many centuries it was also the location for a ferry crossing to the eastern shore of Loch Long, and it is likely that this is what gave Ardentinny its name: it is derived from the Scottish Gaelic Àird an Teine, meaning 'Hill of Fire ', likely named after the beacon that would be lit at the top of the hill that looms over the village to signal a traveller wishing to use the ferry.

It was one group of travellers in particular – the Vikings – that had inspired John to make this pilgrimage. He believed it highly likely that Ardentinny would have been the place where hundreds of ships would have landed, carrying up to 6,000 Vikings who were all slaughtered in a particularly bloody battle with the Scots. John wanted to go back in time and pray for that, but also pray for the consequences of generations of bloodshed in Scotland. He wanted to pray for a break in the violence that still exists in Glasgow, whether that's the sectarian divisions between Catholics and Protestants, or just the way that people would often sort out disputes in pubs through fighting rather than talking.

As a man who had suffered so much emotional violence from his own father, it was easy to see why this prayer in this place meant so much to him.

Unfortunately, a storm blew in as we sailed up Loch Long towards Ardentinny, making it impossible to land. Not only was rain lashing down, but the whole hillside overlooking Ardentinny was - true to its name - covered in smoke from a large fire on the hillside. We couldn't see what was causing it, but it isn't uncommon for wildfires to break out among the grasses in this part of Scotland. The rain beating down on this fiery hillside and the strong gusts of wind from the storm meant that smoke was billowing across the whole area of Loch Long surrounding Ardentinny.

I held the boat at the edge of the smoke cloud, in hazy sight of the beach, and let John begin his prayer. As Matt, Martin and myself joined in, I could sense that in the natural drama of our surroundings, something equally dramatic was happening for two of our crew.

While Matt and I were undoubtedly blessed by the Lord's presence in this time of prayer, something far more profound appeared to be happening for John and Martin as we prayed for a break in generational violence.

The Holy Spirit was resting heavy on these two men who, in their own ways, had lived lives scarred by the generational violence they were now praying against. The prayer soon moved into not just praying for Scotland, but for the whole of the UK and the healing of divisions, one of the main reasons I embarked on this mission in the first place. Despite this, I wasn't receiving what John and Martin were receiving. They received a massive grace, and the Lord healed wounds that they had carried their whole lives, and as we prayed a vivid rainbow appeared across the whole Loch above the smokey air and grey disturbed sea.

I can't remember how long the whole experience lasted: much like mine and Martin's encounter with the Lord in Loch na Droma Buidhe, it could have been minutes, it could have been hours. When we did come to, I tacked Mintaka to turn us a full 180 degrees to head back down Loch Long and towards our overnight stop on the edge of Glasgow, the James Watt Dock Marina near Greenock, on the banks of the River Clyde.

The next morning, we were to sail into the heart of the city to a ceremonial mooring in the city centre, ready for the Celebrate Scotland gathering.

As he packed his bags and prepared to leave the boat, Martin gave me a big hug to say goodbye. He then pulled something out of his back pocket and handed it to me. I looked down at this small, dog-eared book with gaffer tape holding its spine together. It was Martin's Pieta prayer book.

'I want you to have this, ' he said.

'Martin, I can't take the book. This is what's brought you to the Lord. This is what brought you through prison. This is what you pray on every day… I've seen you! '

'I want you to have it. I don't need it anymore.'

Martin's experience at Ardentinny had cemented the grace that we had both encountered at Loch na Droma Buidhe. I took the book for two reasons: firstly, it was clear Martin now had a very personal relationship with the Lord, free from guilt and shame and trusting in his Father in Heaven; secondly, because you can't refuse a guy like Martin.

Matt at the helm, with Ailsa Craig behind us on the horizon

John leading us in praise on our way to Ardentinny

NINE

THE SHOFAR AND SHALOM
(GLASGOW TO LIVERPOOL)

'The Holy Spirit also testifies to us about this. First he says:
'This is the covenant I will make with them after that time,
says the Lord. I will put my laws in their hearts,
and I will write them on their minds.' Then he adds:
'Their sins and lawless acts I will remember no more.'
(Hebrews chapter 10, verses 15 - 17)

THERE ARE CERTAIN PLACES IN THIS WORLD WHERE HEAVEN AND earth seem closer to each other. Ancient Celtic Christians called them 'thin places', where the veil separating the two realms is thinly stretched. Many of the islands off the western coast of Scotland were given this title by those early Christians, including the Isle of Arran and Holy Isle, which we had visited on our way into Glasgow. It was precisely its reputation as a 'thin place' that led St. Molaise to live at Holy Isle as a hermit. I pondered all this after we had visited Holy Isle for the first time on our way into Glasgow, and just as with the tale of St. Cuthbert at Lindisfarne, I felt moved by a deep connection with these men who chose the coast as the place to prepare their missions to establish Christianity across the country. I was also grateful that I had already experienced the 'thinness' of this part of western Scotland through the massive outpourings of the Holy Spirit that we experienced at Loch na Droma Buidhe and Ardentinny.

After our Celebrate gathering in Glasgow – which would take place on Pentecost - I knew we would be once again passing Arran and Holy Isle on our way out through the Lochs and into the Irish Sea. I was keen for my new crew to experience this 'thin place', not least because one of them would be my son Sam.

He was making the journey up from Southampton to join me at Glasgow and sail all the way to Liverpool. It was going to be fantastic to have him onboard, to share what would be some very special moments and memories. I was also very grateful, as I knew what a commitment it was for him to take a whole week off work and spend it away from his young children.

After spending the night in Greenock, I sailed up the Clyde with Martin, John, and Matt to our ceremonial mooring at Yorkhill pontoon, outside Glasgow's Riverside Museum. We sailed into the city praising God at the top of our voices, quite drunk in the Spirit, throwing the boat onto the pontoon with not a worry in the world. As was always the case on this mission, it was an emotional farewell to these new friends of mine, but particularly when it came to saying goodbye to Martin, given our shared experiences and his generous gift of his Pieta.

A small group from Celebrate Scotland was there to greet us at our mooring, which looked across the Clyde to Govan, the city's once world-famous shipbuilding district. We had an impromptu praise and worship session with our departing crew, before heading into the city's parish church of St. Patrick's where a much larger crowd from Celebrate Scotland hosted a three-hour Catholic Charismatic Pentecost vigil.

It was great to see some familiar faces from our intimate gathering in Whitehills, including Ged Farrell, as well as Sam and the two other new crew members who would be joining us for the onward leg to Liverpool via Northern Ireland.

In addition to Sam, crewing the boat out of Glasgow on June 9th – day 44 of the mission – were Mike Baron and Simon (Si) Ireson. Both are involved with Celebrate Birmingham, but given their city's lack of coastal location or tidal river, this was their opportunity to fly the flag for Celebrate in the midlands before a joint gathering of Celebrate Birmingham and Celebrate Northwest in Liverpool. Like John on our journey into Glasgow, Si is a musician, and so was able to accompany our praise and worship on guitar as we sailed along the Clyde and out of the city.

While Mike and Sam were full of enthusiasm for what lay ahead, Si, on the other hand, was in two minds about coming on this mission at all. He had lost his wife about 18 months earlier and was still very much in mourning. He had already called me in the run-up to the mission telling me he had second thoughts about his involvement. I persuaded him that he had made the right choice by signing up, and that he wouldn't regret it. And the Lord made good on my promise to Si at our first stop – the 'thin place' of Holy Isle.

Having left Glasgow late afternoon, we reached Holy Isle in the early evening and were unable to go ashore to visit its retreat centre. Fortunately, despite a rather bleak wet and windy beat all afternoon, the weather brightened up by the time we reached Holy Isle. It was now a beautiful, calm summer's evening, so we anchored for the night off Lamlash, a small fishing village in the bay, in clear sight of the island. With the boat secure, we lifted our hands towards the island and started praying - after all it was Pentecost Sunday, and what a place to be celebrating this feast.

We prayed from the mission prayer scroll, for those who put on the Celebrate weekends and for their intentions. We also prayed for Scotland – for all those I had met so far on the mission, and for the country as a whole. And we prayed for Holy Isle, thanking the Lord for the sacrifice that people like St Molaise had made in the past to bring Christianity to our country. For me, this voyage was about how each of us can, in our own way, live a life of mission, taking the Word to everyone we meet, and Molaise – this little-known saint who I hadn't heard of before I started planning the mission - personified everything about that mission ethos.

As we were praying, this peace came on the boat, just the same as I had experienced with Martin in Loch na Droma Buidhe. Mike started the prayer with a long, resounding blast on his two-foot-long shofar, which he calls Isaiah, as a call to repent and bring victory over the enemy. This traditional Jewish instrument made from ram's horn is used at certain moments in high holidays, such as at the end of Yom Kippur. It is also mentioned throughout scripture.

Its first mention comes in Exodus, on the original Pentecost. Fifty days after Passover, Moses had led the Israelites out of Egypt, through the desert to Mount Sinai. There he would later receive the 10 Commandments, but on that fiftieth day Exodus tell us, having already climbed the mountain twice to speak to the Lord, Moses prepared to do so a third time: 'On the morning of the third day there was thunder and lightning, with a thick cloud over the mountain, and a very loud trumpet blast ' (Exodus Chapter 19, verse 16). That loud trumpet blast in Hebrew is written as the blast of the shofar.

To us Christians, the thunder and shofar blast that went out before Moses received the Law sound very similar to the 'violent wind ' that flooded the Upper Room when the disciples received the Holy Spirit on Pentecost. The writer of the book of Hebrews identifies the Holy Spirit as the fulfilment of Jeremiah's prophecy that one day the Law that Moses received on Mount Sinai wouldn't be written on stone tablets, but on men's minds and hearts (Hebrews chapter 10, verses 15-16).

Here we were, floating in an ancient 'thin ' place, and the Holy Spirit was pouring out onto us, filling up our hearts with the Lord's love as we listened to the same trumpet blast that the Israelites heard across Sinai. It was the perfect way to end our celebration of Pentecost: there was a sense of peace we were feeling that just went deeper and deeper. We had stopped praying out loud – we couldn't speak – as this saturation of joy and peace came over us. It was totally overwhelming, but not crushing. The feeling can be summed up by another Hebrew word: shalom. It is difficult to describe in one word in English, but the way I have experienced it is as the sensation of perfect contentment and peace with where you are right at that moment - a sense of wholeness and tranquillity.

Once again, this feeling of peace came as I sensed the presence of the Lord in the boat with us. But while my previous experiences of his presence at Loch na Droma Buidhe and Ardentinny had come after several days spent together with the crew, this was my first day with my new shipmates. Perhaps this blessing from the Lord at the start of our journey together had come to put Si at ease, to let him know that he had made the right decision and was in safe company? Perhaps it was simply the 'thinness' of this place connecting us with the Lord so quickly? Perhaps I was becoming more attuned to the Lord's promptings as the mission went on, knowing when to pause our sailing for prayer? Or perhaps it was the Lord preparing us for some of the fraught sailing that was to come later on this leg? I don't know. All I know was that evening on Holy Isle, his presence and the sense of shalom was perfect.

After this perfect end to Pentecost, the next morning we prepared to leave Scotland and cross the Irish Sea. We left Holy Isle, first gliding along the coast of Arran and the tip of the Mull peninsula, in view of the eerie and tall rock-stack of an island that is Ailsa Craig. We then continued southwest across the North Channel to the coast of Northern Ireland. We sailed down the cliffy coast with the land starboard, running before a stiff 30 knot breeze and surfing down the waves, eventually arriving at the Belfast Loch in Bangor that afternoon. The Irish Sea can be a tough place to sail at the best of times, so despite a day of relatively good weather and fair sailing, we were all ready for a pint of Guinness and a hot meal in the pub that evening (why does Guinness taste so good in Ireland? Mike is not a drinker, but even he had to agree, one pint wasn't enough).

Bangor was just a staging post on the mission. We had come here to take a route that, while being far from direct, was the easiest and safest way down to Liverpool: down from the Hebrides to Northern Ireland, then across to the Isle of Man and finally into Liverpool.

The sail from Bangor across to the Isle of Man was to provide us with some of our toughest sailing yet: it would take us a day and a half to reach our destination at Peel on the western coast of the Isle of Man, and when we got there we would only have a narrow window of time within which we would be allowed to enter its port.

Peel Harbour and Marina is protected from the ferocity of the Irish Sea by a large man-made breakwater, and tidal flap gates which only allow boats with our draft of two metres to enter an hour or so either side of high tide, and preferably right on high water, due to the silting that had been occurring in Peel harbour. The next high water at which we would most likely be able to arrive into Peel was at 7pm. In a minor sailing miracle, after nine hours of sailing we reached Peel Harbour at 7:05pm, motoring into the silty harbour with 0.2m of depth beneath our keel.

This miraculous arrival at our destination exactly when we needed to be there would happen several times on this mission, and sometimes against all odds.

Despite me being reminded every day that the Lord's hand was on this mission, and that I could trust him, I still found myself up late that night in Peel Marina – like every night – meticulously plotting out the next day's sail while the rest of the crew slept.

The next morning, we were to leave Peel and head south along the Isle of Man coast, eventually rounding the bottom of the island to reach the natural coastal inlet at Derbyhaven, near the Isle of Man airport and our final stop before sailing on to Liverpool. This rounding of the Isle of Man's southern tip can be cut short using a tricky little narrow stretch of water called Calf Sound. This rock-strewn strait runs between the Isle of Man and its smaller neighbouring isle, the Calf of Man, and at just over 600m wide the Irish Sea rushes through it at a rate of knots. Successfully navigating it meant scrapping out of Peel as the tidal height allowed before high water and rushing down to Calf Sound to miss the severity of the tidal streams that cause dangerous wave overfalls.

I planned for it as best as any skipper could and sought local knowledge from Peel's harbour master, but like so much in life, and as with this mission, there comes a point where you must stop planning and preparing, and start doing. And at that point, you must allow yourself to be vulnerable. This intentional vulnerability is an essential part of living a full, spirit-led life. It is a willingness to let go, and let God, to surrender to the unknown and trust in Him. It can mean – as I did through the Calf Sound - overcoming fear and trusting in my navigation and sailing ability to bring a small boat through steep-sided waves the size of commercial vans, with large rocky land masses either side, and a bunch of novices including my own son on board. It can just as easily mean opening up to another person, trusting them with our feelings and emotions. But what I was learning through experiences such as wandering through the streets of Oban with Martin was that, as Christians, perhaps more than anything intentional vulnerability means opening yourself up and being willing to share our faith with others, even strangers. We might be welcomed; we might be rejected or ridiculed… but we might just change someone's life by loving them from a place of spirit and compassion.

Having successfully navigated the Calf Sound with whoops from my crew and a shout of 'we're surfing' as we flew up and down the enormous waves, the rest of the leg around the bottom of the Isle of Man was plain sailing.

We arrived in the bay at Derbyhaven and anchored next to a rocky outcrop called St Michael's Isle, a small island connected to the mainland by a causeway. Sitting on top of St Michael's Isle were the remains of an ancient-looking stone chapel. After a lovely dinner cooked by my crew as a celebration of our sailing heroics, I looked up the chapel on my phone. St Michael's chapel dates back to the 12th or even possibly the 11th century, and despite being 1,000 years old, much of its limestone structure is still standing: the roof is missing, as is the bell from the bellcote at its western end, the windows, and everything inside. But it was still recognisably a chapel despite being bashed by the weather in the Irish Sea for a millennium. What I read next first made my jaw drop open, and then put me in fits of laughter as I tried to tell Sam, Si and Mike the beautiful irony of the spot where we had chosen to shore up before crossing to Liverpool: the chapel, or more to the point the ground all around it was until the 19th century used as a burial ground for two types of people, both of which came worryingly close to describing the four of us on the boat. Firstly, it was the place where the Manx would bury shipwrecked sailors. Secondly, as if that wasn't harrowing enough, the website went on to explain that, from the Reformation onwards, it was also the place where the Isle of Man's Catholic community would bury its dead.

There we were, four Catholic sailors bobbing on the water next to the final resting place of so many who had gone before us. After the initial laughter and exchanges of mock worried looks, we then turned to the only thing we could and should do on this mission: prayer. We prayed for all those buried on the island, thanking the Lord for their lives. We also thanked the Lord for the many blessings so far on this mission, and we particularly asked him to bless our crossing to Liverpool, which we would need to do at night.

Just as with sailing up the Thames into London, entering the mighty River Mersey must be timed to perfection to ride the

flood tide into the city. I checked the chart and saw the best time
to arrive would be early morning, meaning that after supper and
a couple of hours sleep, we would be on our way in the middle
of the night. This wasn't the first time we were sailing at night
on this leg – and I had already done it many times on this
mission - but it's never easy. Doing so requires intentional
vulnerability, trusting in the Lord and what I can see on the
boat's navigation screen.

We thankfully navigated the 70-mile night passage safely,
threading our way through the confusion of lights that marked
out numerous oil rigs and wind farms strewn all over the bay.
Sailing up the Mersey at dawn was quite an experience under
the direction of Liverpudlian Port Controllers, who expertly
guided us in by VHF radio, between the large commercial
vessels in the 12-mile-long narrow channel, into the heart of
Liverpool and its incredible docks.

It was a wonderful time to arrive, the sun was just up but hidden
in a heavy overcast sky, which created a forbidding atmosphere
as we rode the enormous 10m tide into this powerful imposing
dockland city and its world-famous waterfront. The Royal Liver
Building seemed to be watching us sailing in, and I could not
help think she was curious as to why this little boat was there,
and where we had come from.

Once again I had secured a city centre mooring, this time at the
marina run by Liverpool Yacht Club, located next to the city's
iconic Albert Docks. We had arrived two days before the

Celebrate Northwest and Birmingham contingent would stage another gathering for the mission, allowing us time to rest, relax, and be tourists, visiting the city's magnificent Anglican and Catholic cathedrals.

It was a great luxury to spend this time with Sam, Mike and Si while waiting for the gathering before their departure home. We were able to give thanks together in the Catholic Cathedral, and enjoy the warm hospitality of the city's inhabitants, as we ambled about the streets, pubs and restaurants - such a delight after a week of meals limited by Mintaka's small galley kitchen. After the gathering, which again was wonderful to be praising and worshipping out in public, we said our farewells to each other. It was doubly emotional not only to be saying goodbye to my crewmates, but to my son as well. But from what we had experienced on this leg and the many before, I knew there would be many more spirit-filled adventures to come, and that, trusting in the Lord, it wouldn't be long before I soon saw Sam and my grandchildren once again in Southampton.

I had been keen to meet up with the Prince of Peace community based in Liverpool, to discuss participation of Marriage Encounter at their New Dawn conference, and unbelievably a member of their community came to the gathering and invited me to a memorial service that evening for their founder Myles Dempsey. This was a beautiful restorative evening of worship and prayer ministry for me, where I was able to meet and pray with Gary Stevens, their new leader, who had not long lost his son through tragic circumstances. A humbling experience for me as you can appreciate, putting my 'goodbye' to my son Sam into a different perspective.

CREW TESTIMONY
SI IRESON

If you have ever met Russ, you will know that he is a captivating individual. His compelling enthusiasm about the Lord, his family, any of the many movements, events and causes he supports, or indeed his love for sailing, draws you in. I was at the Celebrate team retreat weekend in January 2019 when I first met Russ. He was on a mission, literally, and he wanted people to join him. I was on a journey too. My wonderful, precious wife had died two years previously. Following this enormous loss, the Lord reached out to my brokenness and gently showed me how her passing was not the end, for her or for me. He had plans for my life. It was in this setting that I heard the call from Russ to sail around the UK praying for our country and the Celebrate conferences. I have spent a lot of time on the water, although not in a sailing yacht, and I was instantly drawn to being part of this mission.

It is hard to put across the impact of sharing a small boat with three other men with the constant prayer, singing and eating that accompanied our focus on the sails, ropes, waves and compass. On the first night we sailed around Holy Island and moored up overlooking Lamlash, a small Scottish town in the middle of nowhere. The water was still and silent as we sat and prayed together whilst taking in the incredible creation that God has given to us. The scenery was breath-

taking and God's presence with us was palpable. We sang songs and
Mike blew the shofar. What an incredible sound of God's power, healing
and promise as it resounded over the water. There are not the words to
describe this sufficiently.

Russ has a grace and gift of intercessory prayer, encouraging prayer
for everyone and everything in all that we did. In our journeying I
came to grow in my own appreciation of this. Each of us as we came
into port would be on fire for the Lord as he prepared our hearts for the
people we would meet. People were interested in our mission and
telling people that we were part of this amazing experience was an easy
conversation starter. Russ was full of his stories of the journey and
experience up to this point and we were eager and attentive listeners.
How God was blessing him, all those who were journeying with him
and indeed those people he met.

Russ introduced us to tiffin. Not a term I had heard before, but one I
became fond of. It was basically cake and very welcome it was too with
a mug of redbush tea.

He also introduced us to the most fantastic sailing any of us had
experienced. We sailed around the Isle of Man and in the process had
to navigate between two rocks with very little room for manoeuvre.
The waves were quite significant here and we shot through at a rate
of knots. It was quite the experience, which set us up nicely for the
next 24 hours as we sailed through the night and into Liverpool.
This was the first time that we truly couldn't see land in any direction.
The boat did feel very small at that point, but wow. wow, wow, what
an experience. Coming into Liverpool the following morning was a

sight to behold. Literally ships 'parked ' in the middle of the ocean waiting to enter the harbour, not to mention the oil rigs and wind farms.

Later we were walking by the docks in Liverpool and Mike shared a bit of his testimony with us. We were so moved by his words that we knelt on the pavement and gave thanks to God. We could have been the only people there, and it was such a precious moment.

A walk up to the Anglican Cathedral and they had a huge globe suspended from the ceiling. It was quite a sight and just emphasised the incredibleness of God's creation, leaning on the beauty that had been our backdrop for the past week.

It was quite a shock leaving Russ to continue his journey and to come back home. I was bereft of the precious company and monastic life that we had shared together. This week formed a key moment in my journey with the Lord and I will always treasure it and indeed recommend it to any that have the opportunity to do it or anything like it. I would definitely sign up again given the chance – but I'd bring less luggage next time – hopefully spiritually as well as physically. When we risk, step out and trust, the Lord is there to embrace us in our expression of faith.

*Sam at the helm and Si on the guitar
as we praise our way down the Irish Sea*

Mike's shofar and the prayer scroll

*Skipper and crew enjoying
Guinness in Ireland*

TEN

FOR EVERYTHING THERE IS A SEASON
(LIVERPOOL TO CARDIFF)

'For everything there is a season,
and a time for every matter under heaven:
a time to be born, and a time to die;
a time to plant, and a time to pluck up what is planted.'
(Ecclesiastes, Chapter 3 Verses 1-2)

THIS SAILING MISSION BEGAN FOR ME WHEN I LAY IN BED AND asked the Lord life's big question: what's it all about? It is the kind of question we all ask at various points in life, but particularly during those moments when we are faced with our own mortality, or the mortality of someone we love. As a crew we faced this together during the leg from Liverpool to Cardiff when we shared in a crewmate's grief.

My new crewmates at Liverpool were Gemma Wildsmith, her friend Christine Sterlini, and Yvonne Watts. I have known Gemma for many years through her involvement with Celebrate, first as a youth minister at various regional weekends, then more recently as national coordinator of the weekends while Jenny Baker took a sabbatical. As a part of the Celebrate leadership, Gemma was aware of the mission from an early stage. While she was enthusiastic about the idea, she told me that she had no real desire to step on the boat herself, having never sailed in her life. However, something was telling me – perhaps it was the Lord's elusive voice - that I should persist with inviting Gemma. The first dates I suggested were a no-go, but then – in another Godly intervention - Gemma had a last-minute cancellation that freed up a whole week and tied in nicely with the departure from Liverpool.

We sped out along the Mersey on its ebb tide and soon we were in the Irish Sea heading West, with the North Wales coast on Mintaka's portside. We headed along past its famous seaside resorts of Rhyl and Llandudno in glorious sunshine, watched over by the mountains of Snowdonia.

After a sheepish late-night arrival in pitch black darkness, we successfully picked our way through a long twisty shallow channel in strong wind and entered the marina just south of Llandudno in Conwy. This walled market town – famous for its imposing medieval castle – was to be the place we prepared ourselves and the boat to get through the infamous Menai Strait between Anglesey and the mainland.

The next morning while the four of us were eating breakfast on the boat, Gemma received a phone call. It was her mum. Gemma's sister Lucy had been seriously ill for some time, and her mum was now calling to say that she had finally passed away.

We shared condolences, hugs and tears, and I said to Gemma: 'Well, surely that's it now, that's the mission over for you? You need to get home.' (It was Thursday, and we wouldn't be reaching Gemma and Christine's planned departure point of Milford until Monday).

Gemma's response blew me away. 'I don't think so,' she said. 'Lucy's house is packed, and Mum's got people coming over and she's asked if they can use my bedroom. This has been a special couple of days so far. I've felt so much peace. So, I think I'm going to stay and complete the next few days with you if that's okay.'

'Of course it is!' I replied, through a strange mix of joy, sorrow and confusion. From then on, for the rest of our journey down to Milford Haven, the Lord just surrounded Gemma with the wonder and beauty of his creation – dolphins swam alongside the boat, puffins kept flying past us, and the weather was gloriously sunny. There were a lot of tears, but the Lord was just loving Gemma and holding her in her grief, allowing her to be in a place where she was comfortable to properly grieve, supported by her dear friend Christine and the incredibly loving and selfless Yvonne, who was a joy to be with. It was a privilege to be a part of it.

We set off together to catch the tide through the spectacular Menai Strait bathed in warm glorious sunshine, a blessing from God on us all.

The most notorious section of the Menai Strait for sailors to navigate is the 'Swellies'. This part of the water has shoals, rocks,

surges and even occasional whirlpools. Sailors are aided by all
the pilotage marks that have been added to the water, and
closely follow them in a fashion not dissimilar to an Olympic
slalom canoeist or skier.

To leave the tide-locked Conwy Marina in a strong headwind
and arrive at the Swellies at slack water is a challenge. In truth,
we had arrived a bit late, but took the decision to go for it rather
than wait twelve hours for the next tide. We raced through the
Swellies under a 7-knot tide and shot out like a cork through the
western Menai Strait to Caernarfon. Whoops of laughter and joy
at the ride and the jaw-dropping scenery were coming from the
crew, with the Lord continuing to hold Gemma in his love.

I had booked us a berth at Caernarfon's Victoria Marina, which
sits just on the other side of the town's medieval fortified walls,
built at the same time as its World Heritage site castle. It was an
amazing location and it was where we said goodbye to Yvonne,
who did not want to leave us; many tears were shed for all sorts
of reasons.

Yvonne waved us off from the Castle walls as we sailed out of
Caernarfon in hot sunshine, and out through a gap in the sand
dunes to round Snowdonia. I had spotted a little bay on the
charts earlier that looked like a likely safe haven and
comfortable spot to anchor for the night to give us a shorter day.
It turned out I wasn't the only sailor to think this. As we pulled
in and dropped the anchor, the boat swung round and came
very close to a small boat already in the bay.

An officious-sounding voice in pure Queen's English barked: 'You can't anchor there. Off! Off!' I looked and saw this woman, clearly on her own, standing on her little red boat and waving her hands as if she were shooing us away.

'Oh, sorry,' I said, 'I didn't realise we were going to get so close.' But she just shouted expletives at me, about how I was getting close to her boat. As she was swearing at me, I felt something come over me and the Lord said: 'You need to speak to her with kindness.'

Feeling the peace of the Lord's presence, I was relaxed, but rather cheekily made a joke, which in hindsight wasn't the best idea. 'Do you want me to move... it might be easier for you to move your smaller boat?'

She went ballistic! 'I'm only joking,' I quickly added. 'I will gladly move the boat, of course I will. But I've got something else to ask you.' 'What's that?' she barked back.

I said: 'You're on your own, a long way from the shore... would you like to come aboard our boat for dinner tonight?' She replied in disbelief: 'I've just given you a right rollicking, and you want to make me dinner?!'

'That would be really wonderful,' I said, 'would you do that?' 'Oh, hang on a minute,' she said, looking the boat up and down, 'What if it's true?' Are you going to try and convert me or something?'

I smiled and said: 'Do you know what, we're going to give it our best shot!' She started laughing. We duly moved our boat and then at 7:30pm I rowed over to her in a dingy to bring her over to Mintaka.

Once aboard she started telling us her story. Her name was Gill, and she had recently finished serving in the army. She was now sailing around the UK to spend time gathering her thoughts, trying to decide what to do with her life.

Over dinner and a couple of glasses of wine, we told her about the mission, and Gemma also shared about her sister, which I think touched Gill deeply. By the end of the evening we had prayed with Gill, and there was cuddling and laughter and tears.

What that whole experience with Gill taught me is how wonderful things can happen when we treat others the same way the Lord treats us. The Lord loves us, and we throw it back in his face when we sin. But his response is to love us even more – as St. Paul puts it: 'where sin increased, grace abounded all the more' (Romans 5:20). In that situation with Gill, the Lord was teaching me to love over the top of however I might be feeling. When this woman was getting angry and shouting, my response internally was 'you don't need to swear at me, I can move, just hold your horses and calm down', but I tried to love over the top of the situation. Instead of simply reacting to the situation, I made a conscious effort to respond with love. And the end result was a wonderful experience for all of us.

This experience with Gill was just one of the many ways I was starting to hear the Lord more clearly as the mission progressed. He also spoke to me as a sailor, showing me little miracles and mercies that only I, as the sole experienced sailor on the boat, would notice. The Lord meets us where we are, and he met me in my love of the sea and sailing. He showed me miracles that I would understand around weather changes and around things that went wrong with the boat, which he was able to sort out on many occasions.

After Friday night with Gill, we rose at 4am on Saturday to sail down the Welsh coast for 16 hours. We again passed the magnificent peaks of Snowdonia and saw puffins on the rocks and in the sea. Gemma said that the only thing we were missing to complete the perfect day were dolphins. The Lord duly delivered a large pod of dolphins: they appeared alongside the boat and escorted us across Cardigan Bay, before we headed landwards to the delightful old quay at Fishguard late on Saturday evening. Saturday also happened to be Christine's birthday, and Gemma surprised her that evening with cards and gifts from family and friends that she had smuggled onto the boat.

The next morning, Sunday, was our penultimate day together, and we started the day by heading to Mass in Fishguard's Catholic church. Buoyed by the wonderful events of the last 48 hours, and filled with the Holy Spirit, we walked up into the town, offering prayer for people we met, including an old municipal gardener who in turn prayed for us. On arrival at the church entrance, I announced with a beaming smile full of the Holy Spirit and in a loud voice, 'We're here!' Gemma and Christine laughed, a few parishioners looked at us strangely and the welcomers in the Narthex simply asked, 'Sorry, who are you? Have we missed something?'

After explaining to them, and then to the parish priest, what we were doing, the priest kindly invited me up during his homily to give a short talk about the mission to the whole church. We stayed for tea after Mass and enjoyed meeting most of the parishioners, some of whom wanted to get more involved in the Charismatic Renewal, saying there was not too much going on for Catholics in their part of Wales. We were delighted to make further introductions for them to our charismatic friends in Wales.

It was another wonderful experience brought about by this spirit of openness to the Lord's promptings that was growing in me throughout this mission.

That openness was allowing myself and some of my crew to receive spiritual insights into various nautical things that were taking place. One that really struck me was towards the end of this leg of the mission, as we sailed into Cardiff Bay.

My last day sailing with Gemma and Christine was a rather long, damp, misty and boisterous sail through the notorious Ramsey Sound, The Bitches, around Jack Sound and the island of Skokholm. We hunkered down, grit our teeth and got it done, good stoic character-building sailing. The scenery was lovely I am sure, if we could only see it - I must go back one day and take a second look. I had said many emotional goodbyes on this mission, but none more so than saying farewell to Gemma and Christine at Milford Haven - we had shared something very special.

The next day, I set off alone and sailed for two days, making my way along the Pembrokeshire and Southern Wales coast. After a cracking spinnaker run to the holy island of Caldey, I made an incredibly peaceful anchor stop at the picturesque town of Tenby. After so much time in the company of others, that evening reminded me that a little time alone with God is a good thing. With Mintaka nestled in a protected bay under Tenby, I ate a boat curry on the foredeck in the setting sun and then held my own little prayer vigil into the night. I have never felt so at peace and so close to God, the only boat in the bay, but with Jesus I am never alone.

After Tenby I continued along Wales's southern coast to Swansea, a city that I would visit twice on this sailing mission. The first of these occasions was to collect my now good friends Fran Graham and Ingrid Haupt-Schott to continue the voyage up the Severn Estuary and into Cardiff Bay. Easier said than done: the wind built and we were hunkered down, sailing close hauled into 30-knot winds, before heading inshore to get shelter and a more comfortable passage past Barry into the Welsh capital.

Cardiff Bay is a large body of water formed by a man-made tidal barrage and overlooked by the Welsh National Assembly building, where we would soon be moored for the Celebrate Wales gathering. As we entered the bay, through the most obscure little entrance in the mammoth barrier, right next to the beach (it makes me shudder now thinking how close we were to the beach in an onshore wind), we continued to do battle with a fierce headwind. All the sails were down and I asked Ingrid, who had never sailed before, to just steer the boat into the wind so that we didn't lose control and get blown back onto the rocks surrounding the other side of the bay. Crouched down at the front of the boat, trying to tie on the fenders and mooring lines as water lashed at me from every direction, I heard Ingrid shouting at me over the howls of the wind: 'Russ, I can't control the boat, it's blowing everywhere, the steering wheel isn't working.' The wind was catching the boat and blowing us back over towards the edge of the bay.

I shouted back: 'You've got to put a bit of throttle on, you've got to move the boat forward, because until there's water flowing over the rudder, the rudder does nothing. You can waggle it all you like but it's not going to change the direction of the boat.'

Ingrid quickly gave the throttle a little burst, and suddenly the back of the boat swung round and we were back on course holding into the wind. She then shouted out: 'It's a bit like the Holy Spirit, Russ.' 'I'll speak to you about it in a minute Ingrid,' I said as I fumbled with fenders and lines in the stiff breeze. Now didn't seem like the best time for a spiritual lesson.

'No, Russ it's like the Holy Spirit.' 'All right,' I said as I clambered back into the cockpit having secured the last of the fenders and lines, 'tell me, why is it like the Holy Spirit?' 'Well, unless you move in some direction, even if it's the wrong direction, without the flow over the rudder it doesn't work,' she said.

'And with us, it's no use just sitting still and praying that we will move off in the right direction in our lives. The Holy Spirit can't make us move. You have to put a bit of throttle on, get moving, even if it's completely 180 degrees from where the Holy Spirit wants you to go. You have to start moving, so then the water is flowing over the rudder and the Holy Spirit will bring you back into direction.'

This was possibly one of the biggest spiritual lessons I took away from the mission: that you can't just sit still and say 'Lord, just show me the direction you want me to move in'. He's going to say, 'I will, if you move. If you just go somewhere I'll do it. You must move off somewhere with me in any direction. Don't worry about what direction it is in, I'll take care of that – you've just got to get moving.'

It was a stunning insight and a blessing for us as we neared the end of this eventful leg around Wales. We finally moored up outside the Welsh National Assembly building and then prepared for another Celebrate gathering the next day. I was so looking forward to seeing people who may turn up to our planned gathering, and super-excited that my dear friends

Sue and Charles Whitehead, the founders of Celebrate, would be there; their encouragement and support for the sailing mission was invaluable. The last time I saw them was at the London Gathering at St Katherine's Docks, but this was different: this was in Sue's homeland, the country she loves so much. Sue had been closely following my progress throughout the mission via the Facebook page. Inspired by my testimony of my time with John Wormall at Holy Island, she presented me with a small model of three dolphins leaping out of the water. She named it 'Father, Son and Holy Spirit'. Sue also gave me a packet of Tenby's very own Davies Lossin Dant sweets, as a memento of my vigil in her favourite Welsh town. More importantly, Sue gave me a copy of her new book 'Let Your Light Shine', which included a history of Celebrate and a reference to our sailing mission.

Our prominent position outside the home of the Welsh Parliament attracted a fair amount of attention, with passers-by intrigued by the flags on the boat and our singing swelling, adding to a good turnout of worshipers and musicians for the gathering. Charles and Sue were in fine voice, although Sue was rightly distracted from her singing to talk with people around us and offer prayer. This included extending the offer to a group of rather amused teenagers, before roping in a BBC weather presenter and camera crew who were doing a live broadcast.

It was a great way to prepare for the festivities for the Celebrate Wales weekend, which would be starting two days later in Cardiff.

CREW TESTIMONY
GEMMA WILDSMITH

When Russ told me about his idea for the Celebrate Sailing Mission, I must admit that I thought he was crazy. It sounded like an incredible idea but fraught with complicated logistics and I was worried that he wouldn't get any volunteers to crew the boat with him.

I was reluctant at first to volunteer, having no sailing experience at all, but Russ was persistent. He sent me a few dates, none of which I could make. Something in my diary got cancelled and I suddenly had a whole week that I had to decide how to use. There were a few options, but it felt right to get back in touch with Russ and he said that he was looking for crew to sail with him out of Liverpool and around Wales that week.

I'm so glad that I gave in, as it was such an incredible experience! From the moment we stepped on the boat, which at this point had already been sailing for two months, you could just feel the thick atmosphere of the Holy Spirit's presence. Prayer came quite easily on board, whether it was a spontaneous moment of praise, interceding for the land that we were sailing past, or the moment of affirmation we had in the middle of our last day together, praising God for the gifts we had seen in each other.

My favourite moment was when we were anchoring up in a tiny little bay. A lady on the boat next to us said very angrily that she thought we were too close, and we needed to move. Rather than reply with another heated comment, Russ just looked up and kindly invited her to dinner! She looked rather taken aback but accepted the invitation and we in turn moved the boat further away from hers just to be on the safe side. Gill came over to spend the evening with us on the boat and it was such a beautiful encounter as we all shared something of who we were and why we were sailing.

My good friend, Christine, had also joined us on the boat and even celebrated her birthday on board. I surprised her with some gifts and cards that I had snuck into my bag, and God surprised us with a gloriously sunny day and a pod of dolphins who came alongside swimming and playing for over half an hour. Tragically my sister lost her fight with cancer during this adventure and being out on the water that day, surrounded by the beauty of the Creator, was such a balm for the soul. I felt so at peace and so loved by God despite being in the midst of difficult and painful emotions in my heart.

One thing that the sailing mission taught me is that God can turn our passions into mission, he can take something that we're interested in, and love doing, and use it to build his kingdom and reach out to his people. I'm not sure I really learnt much about sailing, so I'm still a rubbish crew member, but I learnt so much about God, myself and others that I'd jump at the chance to do it again.

Gemma (left) sat next to our sailing neighbour
and dinner guest Gill, and Christine (right)

Arriving in Cardiff Bay
with Fran and Ingrid

Dolphins alongside us
off the Welsh coast

ELEVEN

SURRENDER
(BRISTOL)

*'The Spirit helps us in our weakness. We do not know what we ought
to pray for, but the Spirit himself intercedes for us through wordless
groans. And he who searches our hearts knows the mind of the Spirit,
because the Spirit intercedes for God's people in accordance with the
will of God. And we know that in all things God works for the good
of those who love him, who have been called according to his purpose.'*
(St. Paul's Letter to the Romans,
chapter 8 verses 26-28)

I F OUR ARRIVAL INTO CARDIFF SPARKED A SPIRITUAL INSIGHT ABOUT
needing to move for the Lord to do his work, then my time
spent in its neighbouring city across the Severn hammered
home another lesson I had been repeatedly receiving throughout
this mission: that once we're on the move with the Lord, we must
trust that he will always come through, no matter how unlikely
it seems.

It is a lesson that I first encountered before I had even set sail, when
Storm Hannah threatened to leave all my preparations in tatters.
Slowly, little by little, my trust in the Lord was growing through
these moments of adversity on the mission, as I learnt that he
would always deliver.

My time in Bristol would present me with possibly the most
astounding example of this kind of lesson in the whole mission.

Bristol also showed me how far I had come in being bold for the Lord. After the Celebrate Wales gathering in Cardiff, I sailed to Portishead where my dad, Mike, who lives in nearby Clevedon, turned up to say hello and ended up coming with me and Ann Tarr up the Avon into Bristol city centre. It was Sunday 30th June, and a gloriously sunny day, and to add to the day's splendour we even passed a replica of John Corbet's 15th century ship The Matthew, coming the other way down the Avon. The waterfront pubs and bars were heaving, and revellers were sitting and dangling their legs over the edge of the high stone walled banks of the river, built to contain the Avon's 10-metre-high tide. As we sailed past, some were reading the side of the boat and shouting 'what if it's true' to us. I shouted back 'what's true for you?' Others were simply giving us the thumbs up and shouting, 'it is true, it is true!'

It was a wonderful reminder of how, with the boat's slogan and the flags of the Holy Spirit and Celtic Cross, we were a visible sign of the Lord's presence entering the city.

His presence remained thick and tangible on the boat itself too. This immersion in the presence of the Lord was about to offer me another opportunity to boldly love over the top of another's aggression, just as I had with Gill in Wales at the start of the week.

I had secured a mooring for us at the Arnolfini Centre, a large building dedicated to the arts in the heart of the city's dockland area. It would be here where we would have the gathering for

Celebrate Bristol the following day. The harbour master had cordoned off the area where we could moor and gave me keys to unlock the chains he had wrapped round it. The whole area around the Arnolfini Arts centre was packed with thousands of revellers and, knowing this part of the city stayed open until 3am, I said to Ann and Dad: 'We don't need to stay here tonight. We have the keys for our spot, let's go and find somewhere quieter and come back tomorrow.'

We motored further on around the stone quayside to find what seemed like a far more peaceful place to spend the night. We had a drink on the boat, enjoying the sunshine bouncing off the water, then climbed the ladder of the quay walls to take a stroll. No sooner had I walked onto the quay when three huge men all dressed in black leapt on me. 'What are you doing here?' asked one of them, a large black man who I took to be the leader of this group of security guards.

'I've just parked up here as it's too noisy around the corner,' I said. 'You can't park your boat here, you're backstage at the Elbow concert,' said the boss.

As he was speaking, I heard the Lord say: 'You need to pray with him.' I said to him: 'Listen, we're on this prayer mission around the UK, and the Lord has just told me that I need to offer you some prayer.'

As I'm saying this, far from being filled with faith, I am instead thinking, 'He's going to pick me up by the scruff of the neck and throw me in the water for saying this.'

But instead, he replied: 'You could do that, yeah.' His two colleagues are now looking on in disbelief as I step forward and lay my hand on his shoulder to start praying with him. He tells me his name is Luther, and that he wants prayer for clarity. 'I've been doing this job for years, and I'm not sure it's what I'm meant to be doing,' said Luther. 'I think there's more.'

After the prayer, he opened his eyes and thanked me, then added: 'I'm going back up to London tomorrow to see my mum. I normally get there after she's been to church. But tomorrow I'm going to surprise her, get up there early and go to church with her.'

And with that Luther and his colleagues let me, Dad and Ann go through the concert area, saying to just ask for Luther when we wanted to get back to the boat. The whole experience probably lasted no more than five minutes, but it was such a powerful reminder not only of how to love over the top of someone's apparent aggression, but also how, the more I trusted the Lord, the more I could hear his voice clearly, and the more he would do amazing, unbelievable things.

Despite this, my trust in the Lord was to be stretched to near-breaking point by a technical challenge with the boat that I had to deal with while we were in Bristol.

Ever since Liverpool, the self-steering gear on the boat had been developing a fault. This was a problem, as it was an essential bit of kit for this mission: a self-steering gear allows you to lock the boat onto a certain course. When sailing with a novice crew, or when alone, the self-steering allowed me to go to the front of the boat to do things such as changing the sails. It also meant that during our long days of sailing – the longest would be up to 22 hours in one go – I didn't need to stay constantly on the wheel for the whole journey.

I first noticed something was up with the self-steering when, coming into Liverpool, it locked the wheel by itself. This was the second time it had happened, the first being as we sailed into Peel on the Isle of Man. In Peel it was nothing more than a nuisance that soon fixed itself. However, when it happened so soon again on our journey into Liverpool, I knew we had a problem.

During a stop in Swansea, I took the self-steering unit apart to see what was going on. It was clear that it had failed. This was now a much bigger problem. Not only are self-steering units expensive – around £3,000 – they are also difficult to get hold of. They're not the kind of thing any marina workshop would have just lying around.

I found the manufacturer online and gave them a call. I explained the urgency of my situation, that I had dates I was trying to hit for various Celebrate gatherings and meetings with crew on the mission and asked if they could send me a new unit via a courier. Unfortunately, the voice down the other end of the line replied: 'We don't make that unit anymore and it's specific for your boat. You'll have to send the unit back to us, and it's a six-week turnaround to rebuild the unit.'

This really wasn't an option. I suggested that maybe I could replace one of the bearings that looked the most likely cause of the unit's failure. 'Yeah, you can do that,' replied the manufacturer. 'I've got a bearing here you could have.'

I needed to get my hands on this bearing as soon as possible. 'Where are you based?' I asked. He replied 'Fareham', and straight away I thought, 'Okay Lord, is this the start of a miracle?' Deirdre just so happened to be in Fareham, babysitting for our son Tom's family and was coming up the next day to see me in Bristol, as one of only three times we saw each other over the entire mission.

Now that I had the replacement bearing on its way, I had to extract the failed bearing from the unit. I attempted to do this in Portishead, the day before we were due to sail into Bristol. This was a job easier said than done. Where would I find tools that are specific to going into small holes to extract the bearing off a shaft?

I had become very friendly with the harbourmaster there, so I asked him, and he said: 'There's a guy called Brad that lives in the village. He's a good egg, an engineer, he might be able to help you out.'

It was 6pm at this point, but the harbourmaster assured me Brad would still be around and gave me directions to his workshop. As I arrived there, the man who I took to be Brad was walking away from the workshop and getting into his car.

I shouted out: 'Brad! I've come to see you about a miracle!' 'Pardon?' said Brad, looking at me as though he thought I was drunk.

I explained to Brad about the mission, my problem with the self-steering bearing and the recommendation from the harbour-master, and Brad said: 'Well, there's my workshop, if you can find the tool you're looking for then you can borrow it.'

Another little miracle, as a workman rarely lends his tools, especially to a complete stranger. But I think Brad liked the sound of the mission. I found the tool I needed, headed back to the boat, and it pulled the bearing off beautifully. I was full of joy and thanked the Lord for delivering what we needed on this mission.

The next morning at 9am Brad turned up to pick up his tool, and offered to strip down the whole unit, give it a clean and rebuild it. He returned around lunchtime with a like-new self-steering motor, albeit without the new bearing that Deirdre would be giving to me in Bristol later that evening. I thanked him and asked him how much for all his work.

'No charge,' he said. 'I'm just pleased to help.' I thanked him, called him an angel, took a photo with him by the boat and sang his praises on the mission's Facebook page.

We left Brad in Portishead, sailed up the Avon into Bristol and had our spirit-filled encounter with Luther. Soon after that encounter Deirdre met us, hugged me and handed over the bearing. We had a lovely evening together - not at all hampered by my stowaway father who thought it was a great idea to stay on board with us for the night! The next day was warm and sunny I motored back to the Arnolfini Centre Quay to get ready for the Bristol Quayside Gathering in four hours' time. I was excited to get the new bearing fitted onto the shaft of the self-steering gear and enjoy more time with Deirdre who had come all this way from Southampton to see me.

However, try as I might, I couldn't get this new bearing onto the shaft of the reconditioned unit. I tried warming up the bearing on the stove, I tried whacking it on with a piece of wood, but whatever I tried it just wouldn't align with the shaft. Three hours came and went, meanwhile Deirdre was becoming increasingly irritated as this was the first time we had seen each other in over a month and I've spent all my time fussing over a little metal box.

And I'm becoming increasingly anxious as I know we have some long days of sailing ahead of us around Devon, Cornwall and the Scilly Isles that would be nigh on impossible without functioning self-steering. I pleaded silently with the Lord: 'You've done the whole thing for me, I've done nothing, I've just been a witness to the miracles of the bearing being in Fareham, Brad having the tools that I needed. You cannot have taken me this far for it not to happen? But maybe this is it. Maybe this is the end of the mission because I keep hitting this bearing and it won't go on the shaft.' Deirdre said pray again - she's kind of wise like that, so I did.

Instantly the Lord said: 'Go to that bar and ask for a piece of wood that will fit through the slot, that is machine cut 90 degrees to the end that will fit perfectly into the hole to bash that bearing onto the shaft.'

Seriously? I walked into the bar that the Lord showed me, half in faith, half in sheer disbelief. This is Saturday afternoon by the Arnolfini Arts centre, in the height of the summer, and it is 10-deep at the bar. I wait patiently to get to the front, and a manic barman snaps: 'What do you want?'

'I don't want a drink, I'll come back for one later. This is going to sound strange but the Lord has just told me to ask for a piece of wood of specific dimensions, and it has to be perfectly square at the end with a machine cut.'

He stayed silent for a moment, that seemed like an age, and as I was about to walk or run away, he said: 'Funny you should ask; there is a woodworking class that uses our storeroom next to the art college behind us. Let me see if they can help with what you're looking for.'

Within 45 seconds he had disappeared then returned with a machined piece of wood that was the exact size I was looking for. I thanked and blessed him profusely, returned to the boat and put the piece of wood into the bulkhead hole onto the steering unit. I tapped it once and the bearing slid gracefully onto the shaft. Just ridiculous and miraculous.

Yet again, the Lord had taken me to the point of dismay and despair. But instead of giving up hope, he showed me that what I needed to surrender was my fear, and my need to be in control. Even when all seemed lost, he was there working things out for us.

Above all, what that Saturday in Bristol showed me was the importance of staying in prayer. When you stay in prayer, you can't help but love the people in front of you. This allowed me to see past people like Gill and Luther's aggression. But staying in prayer, feasting on his Word, was also finally enabling me to hear the Lord's voice, to follow his promptings and to see miracles like the self-steering repair occur.

Brad, who helped save the mission in Portishead.

Arriving at a busy quay in Bristol

Celebrate Bristol gathering outside the Arnolfini Arts centre

TWELVE

WHERE THE WIND BLOWS
(BRISTOL TO SCILLY ISLES)

'The wind blows wherever it pleases. You hear its sound,
but you cannot tell where it comes from or where it is going.
So it is with everyone born of the Spirit.'
(John, Chapter 3, Verse 8)

THE GATHERING AT BRISTOL WAS TYPICALLY JOYFUL, BUT ALSO distinctly ecumenical: as well as folk joining us from the local Catholic Charismatic community linked to Bristol Celebrate, we had a lovely turn-out of our Anglican brothers and sisters, who had joined us from my dad's parish of St. Andrews in Clevedon. They were there to accompany their vicar Trevor Crenshaw, who was so excited about our mission that he wanted to do more than just attend a gathering. He had sought and been granted permission by the Bishop of Bath and Wells to join us for a few days on the boat.

After a wonderful afternoon gathering rolled into Sunday evening, Trevor arrived back at the quay the next morning to climb aboard. I had said farewell to Deirdre, Ann and Dad at the gathering the night before, and in their place as crew was now Trevor and Dan Burgess. Dan was a young dad, a similar age to my sons, and like them he had grown up with Celebrate, particularly the week-long event in Ilfracombe, and we had become close over the years.

It was Ilfracombe where I hoped we would be heading next. It

would be a symbolic return, with no gathering planned and my
schedule allowing us to stay just one night if we were to make
it to Plymouth in time for the next gathering. I just hoped we
would be able to do so: the coasts of north Somerset, Devon and
Cornwall are notoriously rough and rocky in places with little
shelter or safe havens.

But before we faced that, we had the wonderful experience of
sailing back down a sunny, if slightly blowy, River Avon. We
passed the sights and sounds of Bristol, including sailing
beneath the engineering marvel of Clifton Suspension Bridge,
and then returned to the Severn Estuary once again. We hugged
the shoreline past Portishead, then eventually Clevedon came
into view, with Trevor's congregation once again out in full force
and cheering us on.

The sun was shining, the boat's self-steering was working and
we were brimming over with the Holy Spirit… what could
possibly go wrong?

As I said, it had been a bit blowy on the Avon coming out of
Bristol, but as we left the relative protection of the river, and then
the Severn Estuary, what had been occasional gusts became
full-blown strong winds out on the open seas. We hadn't long
begun sailing along the north Somerset coast when disaster
struck: the main sail ripped.

I had to sail the boat close to the coast from Minehead,
attempting to get some shelter in the lee of the cliffs. This soon

proved itself to be a futile strategy, as the wind was coming from the opposite direction, straight off the southern coast of Wales.

Poor Dan and Trevor were clinging on for all they were worth as they tried to use gaffer tape to put the sail together while I held the boat tight into the cliff off Minehead. Eventually I shouted to them over the howl of the winds: 'It's too windy with this repair in the mainsail to carry on along the Devon coast. We're going to have to head up, across the Severn Estuary to Wales.'

We managed to sail across the Severn, with waves breaking over the boat and into the cockpit, then resorted to motor sailing to claw our way along the Welsh coast to get to a marina in Swansea before they shut the cill gate at 8pm. Dan absolutely revelled in it, attaching his Go-Pro cameras all over the boat to get shots of the waves, grinning from ear to ear, as he helmed the boat. Trevor, meanwhile, was feeling seasick.

Once again, just as with Peel on the Isle of Man, we made it to the marina with only minutes to spare. It had been a long, exhausting day of 74 miles of rough sailing, and each of us felt it, but especially Trevor: despite being a relatively experienced sailor compared to my usual novice crewmates, the extreme conditions had made him very unwell. It was an inauspicious start to our journey from Bristol, and sadly things were to get worse before they would get better.

The next morning we set sail for Padstow on the north Cornwall coast, another long day with 76 miles of sailing ahead of us. And once again we had a hard deadline: the marina at Padstow closed its lock gate at 7:45pm.

I told Dan and Trevor that we needed to leave before 8am to give ourselves 12 hours to make the journey. 'To do 76 miles in that time,' I told them, 'we will have to average six and a half knots, but the boat only goes at five and a half knots on the motor... I can do more if we sail and the wind's right.'

We came out of Swansea and the wind was dead. I put the motor on as hard as I could, but travelling at five and a half knots meant that for every hour we were at that speed, we would need to make further increases on the average speed to get to Padstow in time. If we didn't reach Padstow before the marina gate shut, then we would have to anchor off or just keep going all the way down the Cornish coast and round Land's End, which would mean the three of us spending two whole days at sea.

We had passed Lundy Island and were approaching the north Devon coast – just under halfway between Swansea and Padstow – when disaster struck: the boat's motor started making horrible erratic vibrations and groaning sounds, before stopping completely.

This left us drifting uncomfortably near a headland on the north Devon coast in light air. Dan and Trevor were sitting ahead of me, enjoying the calm sunny day and blissfully unaware of what was – or wasn't – happening beneath the waves.

As calmly as I could, I said to them: 'Guys, we have a little bit of a problem. The motor has stopped, there's no wind, and we are now drifting with the tide towards those rocks.'

As their smiles disappeared and their eyes widened with terror, I tried to reassure them by adding: 'But we won't let that deter us. So, before I call the RNLI to come and rescue us, why don't we pray and praise the Lord? We'll pray for wind to get us moving.'

We started to pray and a little zephyr of wind came. I thought 'that's interesting', then said, 'I think we need to up the prayer a little bit more chaps.'

We started praying for all we were worth. And as we got closer to the headland, funnily enough the singing went up higher and louder, and the prayer got a little bit more fervent as the rocks neared into view.

But then, at the peak of our prayer, the wind came up, and not in the direction that had been forecast. Instead, it came around the back of the boat on the stern quarter, and soon picked up to a speed of about 15 knots. We put the spinnaker up and did between eight and 10 knots from that point all the way into Padstow.

We were still cutting it fine – it was around 7:30pm by this point – and I radioed the harbour master saying, 'I think I'm going to make it; can you just tell me exactly when you are going to shut the lock?'

The harbourmaster's voice came back over the radio: 'Mintaka, you have 10 minutes.'

I think I'm 15 minutes away,' I replied, 'can you hold it open until then?' I neglected to mention that I had a problematic engine – hoping that when we dropped sail that it would start up okay.

I sailed Mintaka right up to the entrance of the harbour, then tried the engine: it turned the propeller just enough to park the boat, before failing again, just as the lock gates closed behind us. The boat was silent. There were no whoops or cheers. We just sat in the cockpit and looked at each other. We simply couldn't believe the set of circumstances that had led us there.

Reverend Trevor had to leave us the next morning to get back to his congregation, so we celebrated the eventful trip with a hearty meal, intercessory prayer and a good night's sleep. This left Dan and me to face the next leg together. We were super-keen to take in the Isles of Scilly as a must-see place, before rounding England to continue East. We set about finding an engineer to sort out the engine, which we did, filters were changed, and the engine seemed to be running fine again in neutral.

Crossing to the Scillies meant going through the busiest shipping lane of the mission after the English Channel, located off Land's End. While not a world-beater like the Dover Strait, this passage past the bottom of the British mainland is still one of the busiest routes in Europe and is governed, like the Channel, by strict rules on how to cross and avoid collisions in the shipping lanes.

No sailor in his or her right mind would consider going through there without an engine, and the work done in Padstow seemed to have fixed the problem, although the engineer was not completely confident that he'd found the cause of the problem. After we had said goodbye to Trevor, I looked at the weather forecasts and could see the wind would be perfect to sail overnight to the Scillies.

And so, that afternoon, Dan and I headed out of Padstow – the motor again spluttering for just long enough to get us out of the marina – and into a night of sailing under spinnaker for a 70-mile passage to the Scillies.

Dan seemed to have had complete confidence in my sailing ability and did not question whether the grumpy engine was a reason to be concerned, seeing the whole exploit as adventure. Any sailors reading this will be cringing now at my decision, but it seemed okay to me at the time, maybe because I knew Dan was a game lad and that the forecast seemed to support the crossing under sail. We sailed with the spinnaker up, pulling us along nicely at a speed of 8 knots into the darkness. Dan had been uncharacteristically quiet on the trip but this time together alone, under the beauty of the starry night sky, sailing down the blackened Cornish coast, created a wonderful opportunity to share with each other about life and love. We finished talking and the boat then fell silent for several hours. Just after midnight Dan slipped away into a deep sleep in the cockpit, leaving me to reflect on the conversation and concentrate on flying the spinnaker while keeping a lookout for any other shipping. It was an unusually cold night.

We reached the Land's End shipping lanes at 2am and sailed into them using a combination of sight and our AIS system to dodge the ships.

As dawn broke, the wind dropped and after 20 hours of sailing we reached the Scilly Isles. I sailed right into St Mary's Road and dropped the anchor in the relative shelter of St Mary's Pool, checked the holding, thanked God for getting us there safely and fell into my bunk in a deep sleep. These islands south of Cornwall are the closest the UK gets to being tropical, with white sand beaches and crystal-clear seawater. Rested and refreshed, that afternoon I took advantage of these clear waters and swam under the boat to check the propeller. I spotted the problem straight away: wrapped around the propeller was the remains of a fishing net, which seems so obvious now. I told Dan the problem, and he jumped into the water with me. Together we cut at and untangled the net until the propeller was free.

While we were thankful for the wonderful experiences of the wind getting up off Lundy Island and staying good for us all the way to Padstow and then to the Isles of Scilly, we were equally thankful that we wouldn't have to rely solely on the wind for our journey back to the mainland and the final leg of the mission. The next 24 hours on the Scillies with Dan were true elation: we walked all over the sun-baked tiny islands, visited churches, prayed with workers in tea shops, and just revelled in the love of our friendship.

Mintaka moored in Padstow

Dan relaxing after we made it to the Isles of Scilly

Enjoying the sheer beauty of my surroundings in the Isles of Scilly

THIRTEEN

THE DELUGE
(PLYMOUTH)

'My sheep listen to my voice;
I know them, and they follow me.'
(John's Gospel, chapter 10 verse 27)...

SOUTHAMPTON MAY HAVE BEEN THE FINAL DESTINATION FOR THIS mission, but it was Plymouth where I finally arrived at what set me on this journey. It was Plymouth where that ability to hear the Lord, to know him, came fully alive in me. There were of course powerful moments throughout the mission, from the fender board in Ramsgate, to God getting in the boat with me and Martin in the Hebrides, to the miracle of the self-steering in Bristol.

However, it was during the 24 hours that I spent on my own in Plymouth that the Lord immersed me in such a deluge of prayer, it felt as though everything in the mission had been leading up to this point.

After the Scillies, Dan and I sailed to Falmouth where we picked up Tanya Trevener and her teenage children, Jacob and Stephanie. Dan was meant to leave us at Falmouth, but he was having so much fun that he rearranged his plans to stay onboard with us for the weekend, sailing up the southern coast of Cornwall and into Plymouth.

We arrived in Plymouth on Sunday evening and anchored in the fabulous Cawsand Bay just inside Plymouth Sound, rowed ashore for fish and chips and lost Dan and Jacob to a local pub. Dan had to leave us to get home for the start of the working week, and we said our farewells at Plymouth Marina. The hug and parting words were incredibly emotional. We'd had an amazing adventure together, the thrill of it and depth of bonding, like father and son, could never be expressed in words. Little did I know that this was to be a final farewell, I shall treasure the moment forever. (Dan did attend the home-coming event in Hamble at the end of the pilgrimage, but with so many people there and so much excitement, our greeting and goodbye was really fleeting, as one in the crowd. Thankfully, our farewell in Plymouth was very spiritual, intimate, and deeply moving.

Plymouth was Tanya, Jacob and Stephanie's stomping ground, so they also left the boat for the comfort of their own beds before returning to sail around Plymouth Sound ahead of the Celebrate South West gathering the following evening. It was a privilege to sail with this family of God. Tanya is a woman of deep peace and gentleness, with a passion for God's creation and the sea, with childlike enthusiasm to bring people into a loving relation-ship with Jesus. She must have taken 100s of pictures, and never stopped smiling.

This left me on my own for Sunday evening and most of Monday on a spiritual high. I had now been travelling around Britain for over two months – 10 weeks to be precise – and after visiting so many towns, I found I could very quickly pick up a sense of whether it was a place where the work of the Lord was active, a place where I could sense his presence strongly. As I wandered around the quay in Plymouth that Sunday evening, I could feel straight away that this was a place where he was really blessing the work that was going on – and this was before I had spoken to local Christians about all the different outreach programmes taking place in the city.

And Plymouth is a town that needs prayer and good deeds. It is unrivalled in its place in British maritime history, at least as far as the navy is concerned. It was home to the first royal naval base in the 16th century, and it was from Plymouth that the fleets set sail to defeat the Spanish Armada, not to mention being the launching point for the exploits of Sir Francis Drake and Sir Walter Raleigh. By the mid-20th century its main docks, known as Devonport, were the largest in Western Europe, home to frigates and nuclear submarines alongside all manner of commercial vessels, with tens of thousands employed in the dockland area.

However, today that number has dwindled to just a couple of thousand jobs, and certain areas of the city bear all the scars of socio-economic decline common in many of Britain's cities in the post-industrial era. Despite the continuing presence of the Royal Navy, Air Force and Army, Plymouth's economic decline is such that some parts of the city are lined with boarded-up shops, and rough sleepers lie in the doorways.

This deprivation wasn't immediately on view in the genteel

surroundings of the harbour, with the old stone buildings surrounding it converted into plush apartments. However, walking around the quay, I began to sense both how much this place was being covered in prayer, and just how much that prayer was needed.

I found a pub with live music and wandered in. With music, you can instantly become part of the community: you're not just talking to people randomly, you're singing with them and putting your arms around strangers. Within five minutes I had come between two women who had started fighting, and calmly did my best to diffuse the situation. After the ruckus had died down, I got chatting with a guy called Kevin who, to put it mildly, was going through a difficult time. His ex-wife was part of a family who were heavily into dealing drugs. He'd separated from her and the family were trying to get to him and hurt him. I prayed with him in the pub, then prayed with another guy for a disability caused by a leg injury. I then walked out of the pub and immediately found myself talking then praying with another three people, outside a fish and chip shop.

Eventually I wandered back to the boat, saying a little silent prayer of thanksgiving for the evening: 'Lord, you just keep presenting people to me so that I can pray with them. This is amazing.'

The next morning I woke up and hastily made my way across town for an interview with Dave Simpson, who runs a Christian radio station in Plymouth called Cross Rhythms.

On my way there, I walked down into an underpass, where I saw a man using a spray gun to jet-hose the floor. He was cleaning up blood. I asked him what had happened, and he explained that a young lad had been stabbed the night before. I asked the cleaner if I could pray with him. Together we prayed for the stabbing victim, and then I prayed for the cleaner. I later found out that the young man who had been stabbed survived, which was a miracle considering the volume of blood left on the underpass floor.

I reached Cross Rhythms at 9am for an interview with Dave Simpson, the station manager who also presents the afternoon radio show. What was meant to be a 30-minute pre-recorded interview eventually became a whole morning chatting with Dave as he lapped up all my wonderful tales from the mission.

'I'm going to make this a series,' he said, which he duly did, broadcasting six episodes over six weeks. I then headed back to the marina to move the boat, as I had secured a prominent mooring on the Barbican quay for that evening's Celebrate gathering. While at the marina, preparing the boat for the short motor around the corner to the Barbican, I got chatting to a man called Clive. He was admiring the boat, so I told him about the mission and eventually ended up praying with him and his wife for their marriage. Shortly after, Paul Leather from the local BBC came down to see me on the boat for a 20-minute interview, then not only stayed and prayed with me all afternoon, but also treated me to a fish and chip supper on the quay. I remain in contact and friends with Paul to this day, he is a great lad, I am sure there is joint ministry work for us to do that the Lord has already prepared.

After that prayer, I took the boat across the quay to the Barbican, a fantastic old, cobbled street area, and the perfect location for the Celebrate South West gathering that evening, through kind permission of the harbour master.

Just as in Bristol, the gathering was large and it was ecumenical. As we sang and praised, passers-by became bystanders and then swelled the group so that it became a crowd. We had three Catholic priests with us leading the worship, and as we sang, two of them set off into the crowd to pray with people.

It was perhaps the most powerful, most blessed experience of all the gatherings. It felt like we spent the whole night singing together, but eventually the crowd dissipated and people started to go home. As the crowd thinned out at about 10pm, I spotted several guys - the kind you might find in any city centre up and down the country - just wandering around aimlessly.

However, it turned out these guys weren't the same as those you might find in other city centres. It wasn't drugs and addiction that was giving them their gaunt and lost appearance. It was a condition sadly common to military towns like Plymouth: they were suffering – I later found out - from Post-Traumatic Stress Disorder.

Two of them came over to look at the boat, and I started talking with them... 'Guys, are you interested in the boat?'

'Yeah, it looks good,' said one of them who introduced himself as Jim. 'What's all the flags about?'

I told them about the mission, and they told me a little about themselves. Jim used to be in the Royal Navy, while Tez, his companion, was in the Army. Tez was very far-gone in his condition, while Jim just seemed anxious, mumbling his words through his toothless mouth.

I said to them both: 'Do you want to come for a trip tonight?' 'Yeah, great,' came the reply from Jim while Tez nodded. They got on the boat and I motored them around the harbour, just a little jaunt back to the marina berth for the night.

I could see that Jim wanted to go further in his story and would be open to prayer, but Tez was too far gone, his condition meaning he was constantly distracted by every little thing.

I thought, 'I'm never going to be able to properly pray for Jim because the two of them are together', and it was dark by this point, so I just thanked the Lord for this moment.

'Lord it's great to be with them,' I prayed. 'And it was great to pray with them. That's enough for me. Thank you.'

I parked the boat up and, just as I tied the ropes on, up popped Clive who I'd prayed with earlier in the day.

'Hi, did you have a good day?'

'Yes, Clive, we have had a great day thanks. And I've got a couple of new crew who I met on the quayside.'

I didn't know this at the time, but Clive was also in the Army. He immediately recognised Jim and Tez as suffering from PTSD. And he said to Tez, 'Do you want to come and see my boat?'

I didn't ask Clive to do this, but he did. He and Tez wandered off to - as I found out from Clive the next day - have a cup of tea on Clive's boat before heading off in their separate directions.

That left Jim and me alone together on the boat, just as I had prayed.

Jim started telling his story, and said to me, 'I've got no teeth because I've got a face that people like to punch'.

This was nonsense - despite the lack of teeth, Jim was a good-looking guy. I said: 'Jim, your face is beautiful. You haven't got a face that people want to punch.'

'I don't belong anywhere; you know that?' The depth of Jim's feeling of unworthiness and unbelief in himself was just staggering. The reason he had been punched many times had nothing to do with what his face looked like, and everything to do with where he put his face. Like others with PTSD, he would wander around the quay aimlessly at night, running into the wrong crowds as they came out of pubs and clubs.

As Jim told me this, we started to pray. He told me he was

riddled with guilt about things in his life. He said he knew that God is there, but he's too far away.

'He's too far away because I've done too many bad things in my life.'

We prayed through all of this, and at the end of it, as I felt the Holy Spirit again coming down heavily on the boat, Jim gave himself to Christ.

Had I not prayed with Clive, had Clive not been in the Army, had Clive not happened to be on the quay when I pulled up with Jim and Tez, that very special and blessed moment with Jim would never have happened. These aren't coincidences. Throughout the mission, the Lord kept lining things up time and time again to enable these deep prayer experiences to occur with people. It was just beautiful. This deep prayer with Jim was the perfect culmination of all those prayers of love, forgiveness and healing that I had been blessed to share in over the three months of the mission. And it showed me that this was what the gift of hearing the Lord is for. The more I stayed in prayer, and the more I put myself in situations where the Lord could reach those who needed him, the louder and clearer his voice became.

Dan and Stephanie at the helm, with Tanya (left) and Jacob (right)

*Praying on the street
in Plymouth*

*On Cross Rhythms Radio
with Dave*

PART THREE

HOME AND BEYOND

FOURTEEN

DREAMS AND VISIONS

'In the last days, God says,
I will pour out my Spirit on all people.
Your sons and daughters will prophesy,
your young men will see visions,
your old men will dream dreams.'
(Acts Chapter 2, verse 17)...

WHEN YOU START TO HEAR GOD'S VOICE CLEARLY, IT STAYS with you... at least for a while. In the days and weeks that followed those extraordinary 24 hours in Plymouth, I was listening to and speaking with the Lord regularly. His words were coming through crystal clear, and it wasn't just the odd word here and there, as it tended to be earlier in the mission: they were coming through in fully-formed sentences.

I remember how, even several months after the mission, I found myself dancing around my Dad's living room like an idiot in response to my latest chat with the Lord. My Dad, Mike, was upstairs taking an afternoon nap and I was downstairs praying. I heard the Lord say: 'Russ, I want you to dance for me.' He was still pushing me - just as he did with Storm Hannah, with the self-steering mechanism, and on countless other occasions - stretching the limits of my faith so that I grew deeper into Him. And so I happily pranced about, full of the Holy Spirit and on fire for the Lord. To this day I try to stay in a state of prayer to hear what the

Lord has to say to me, but it's not always easy with the daily distractions that I was blissfully free from while on the mission.

It took me four days to sail back to Southampton from Plymouth. It was a leg that brought the mission full circle in more ways than one: Paul Langford re-joined me in Plymouth to help bring Mintaka back into the Solent. Joining me and Paul just for the journey from Plymouth to Dartmouth were Alan and Maria McCarthy, the latter describing her day trip as having 'profound spiritual significance' (*read Maria's testimony in full in 'Further Crew Testimonies', page 158*).

Paul and I then sailed on from Dartmouth to Weymouth, where we welcomed our youngest crew of the mission: my neice Millie-Rose, and Jasmine de Kretser. Despite being just 19, Jasmine was at the time running her own 350-person annual charismatic Christian weekend called 'Stay Awake' in between her university studies. It was such a joy and privilege to pray with her as we glided along the stunning Jurassic Coast into my home waters of the Solent protected by the Isle of Wight.

Had I come this far so soon? I was beginning to get emotional and strangely serene, rather than excited. Arriving at Lymington I once again bid farewell to Paul, as well as Millie and Jasmine. Joining me for the final stretch to home were my fellow Celebrate Southampton team members Angela Slattery and her son-in-law David Barnsley-Parsons. We sailed to the Isle of Wight to spend the final night of the mission in Cowes, before sailing down the Solent to Hamble quay on Saturday 13th July.

We had done it. Or more accurately, the Lord had done it: my many crew members and I had circum-navigated the UK in 77 days and taken part in 12 gatherings around the country, never missing a date. Any experienced sailor will tell you that just doesn't happen. The weather is so incredibly varied and unpredictable on this island of ours – there's a reason us Brits talk about the weather so much – that the chances of avoiding any kind of weather delay while sailing for such a sustained period are slim to none. And yet, the Lord provided, like he always does.

The only kind of delay we suffered had been right at the start, courtesy of Storm Hannah. How different it was now returning to Hamble, grey and blustery when we left, but now bathed in glorious sunshine. Just as on our departure, family, friends, fellow Celebrators and the local BBC radio crew were there to welcome us on our return.

I gave Deirdre a great big hug as we were reunited, before saying hello to so many of the mission's supporters, while Deirdre gave an interview about her excitement at seeing my return that would be played on the next morning's radio.

I was so thankful that we had arrived safely and on time. It was a blessing in itself, but it also meant that I would be able, the following weekend, to attend a charismatic men's weekend - Harvesters - of which I am also part of the organising team.

The Lord clearly wanted me to be there too: this event is a

once-a-year event where men from all around the country –
Catholic, Anglican and other denominations – gather from
Friday evening to Sunday afternoon for a time of prayer and
fellowship. Each weekend has a couple of speakers who are
invited to give talks on the theme of that year's weekend. In
2019, our chosen theme was 'Empowered to Witness', taking the
second chapter of the Acts of the Apostles as its inspiration.

Our main speakers were due to be a Scottish ex-prisoner and a
Polish archbishop. However, upon my return to Southampton I
learnt that due to a personal crisis the ex-prisoner could no
longer come, and the Polish archbishop had broken his arm and
also had to cancel. My fellow Harvesters organisers asked me if
I would step in to give a talk about my experiences on the
mission. I'm no public speaker, but I was happy to fill one of the
slots to share the wonderful time I had spent with the Lord over
the previous months. But that still left several speaking slots
across the weekend that would need to be filled by a far more
experienced and noteworthy orator than myself. I chatted about
it with Deirdre, and she said: 'You should ask Yinka.'

Yinka Oyekan is pastor of The Gate church in Reading, and a
long-time friend of the Celebrate conferences, right back to the
days of the national event in Ilfracombe. However, Yinka is also
a much-in demand speaker at Christian events across the world,
and at that time was president-elect of the Baptist Union of Great
Britain. I expressed my doubt to Deirdre, saying it would be
highly unlikely he would be free the next weekend to come and
speak at an event last minute. But, knowing by now to put my

worldly-scepticism in second place to the God of surprises, I called Charles Whitehead – then chairman of Harvesters – and said, 'Have you thought about asking Yinka?'

Charles replied: 'I have, and funnily enough so have the other members of the team – they all came back with Yinka's name.' Charles phoned Yinka, and he was on a mission in Belgium. However, he was flying back on the Saturday of the Harvesters weekend and said he would be delighted to speak.

I gave my talk about the mission, focusing on the theme of following your dreams, and had a prophetic word, 'just sign up' which unfortunately did not resonate with anyone, but it was a powerful Spirit-filled session anyway. As this was all so last-minute there had been no opportunity for Yinka and I to compare notes on what we were going to say. But, funnily enough, Yinka had chosen the theme of realising your dreams, and during his talk, laid out sheets of paper on the stage, then challenged the men to come forward and 'just sign up' to your dream - astonishing! Twenty-three men came forward and signed up to pursue their dreams. An event that is normally a year in the making was thrown into chaos a week before it was due to take place, only for the Lord to pull it all together at the last minute. Once again, he had left us hanging; then came through at the last.

Those talks on that Harvester's weekend have borne many fruits: Yinka and I started working on several projects together, which led me later in 2019 to join him at several outreach events, one of which was in Switzerland (a whole other story) and support an on-line course in personal transformation. It also led to the creation of this book, as John McKenna, another member of the Harvester's organising team and a journalist, insisted the story of this mission had to be written down and he was willing to do it, as a dream of his own was to write a book.

What neither Yinka, I, nor John, as he began writing this book, could foresee was that so many of the freedoms we took for granted, the freedoms that helped make the mission such a wonderful experience, would soon be taken away from us. Coronavirus came in 2020 and with it disappeared the ability to gather in public, to spend time with strangers, to sing, and even to attend church.

As the world slowly recovers from this awful virus – which Deirdre and I contracted but successfully recovered from in late 2020 – I hope and pray that we embrace those freedoms we once took for granted. Now, more than ever, is the time to seize those freedoms and pursue your dreams. Start planning your adventure for the Lord now, as you never know when the ability for you to do so could be taken from you.

But if, perhaps inspired by this book, you do want to follow your dreams and go on your own adventure for the Lord, how do you know he is really behind it? How do you know this is truly what you should be doing, and not just some personal fantasy driven by ego? Well, the truth is, as my experience taught me, you can never truly know. You must step out in faith. As Ingrid told me as we sailed into Cardiff, just move in some direction, any direction, and the Holy Spirit will soon get hold of you and set you on the right course.

However, that doesn't mean there's nothing you can do to discern whether a dream is from the Lord or not.

As events unfold when you set out on your adventure, look out for tell-tale signs that the Lord is in what you are doing. For me, above all else, it was the energy I seemed to find from nowhere to do everything that was required to put this mission together. It took some doing to complete this prayer mission in 77 days: keeping to a schedule of stopover locations and dates for crew changes and the 12 Ceremonial Quayside Gatherings, arriving home on the exact day I had planned, battling no wind, too much wind and breakages. Pulling in most nights to a different harbour, negotiating prime positions on each quay, keeping in touch with the next set of crew arranging their pick up points along the way, BBC interviews, local press and radio interviews, daily Facebook postings, stocking up the food for the boat between crew changes, daily safety briefings for each different crew, sailing all day, praying and praising all day, praying with people during our walks ashore, repairing and servicing the boat (I had to do three engine oil and filter services), keeping in contact with the family, preparing the welcome meal for the new crew, arranging the twelve main ceremonial quayside gatherings as we went.

All of this should have been exhausting but it wasn't. I would get to my bunk after midnight most nights after doing the next day's navigation and voyage Facebook posting, then up again just after sunrise to get some exercise on my folding bike, food shop and fuel the boat, and get ready to depart and catch the tide after breakfast with the new crew. Where did this energy come from? Not from me. I believe it was from the Holy Spirit, it was supernatural: I was surely listening to God and doing what I was prompted to do - quite remarkable really, and a good test of whether I was doing God's will, following his plan for me.

Over the course of a few years, from first having the idea of the mission to finally completing the journey, I discovered that I had experienced six tests that Christian author Sheridan Voysey summed up in a blog online. These six tests provide a way to discern if a dream or prompting was truly from God and his Holy Spirit:

Six tests to discern a dream
1. The Test of Love
The dream is not about me, my significance, fame, or even my benefit alone. The dream is about God. The dream is about others. I'll benefit from it alright, but it may also cost me significantly. God is love and his ultimate command is to love. My dreams must be sifted through love to ensure it isn't just the result of ego alone.

2. The Test of Time
The dream lingers. Does it quietly pursue me? It isn't one of

many ideas, but the one idea that rises persistently above the many. I like dreaming up new ideas and ventures yet find many of those dreams evaporate over time. The dream needs to be the one dream that will not leave me - even for years - for it to be God's whisper to me.

3. The Test of Peace

It's okay that I feel excited about the dream, even overwhelmed or fearful. But as I pray about the dream is the dominant sense I have one of 'deep peace'? Do I feel passionate rather than driven? The dream may be vitally important but surely I shouldn't be burdened in my spirit. I must be honest and discern if there is a deep prayerful peacefulness that comes with this dream.

4. The Test of Faith

Is my dream bigger than me, my abilities and resources? While it should be in line with my giftings and talents, the dream must take me beyond my level of ability. I won't be able to achieve it without God and others. I feel vulnerable at times at the thought of it all falling in a heap, and this is okay: it means the dream will only be possible by faith.

5. The Test of Confirmation

Some people who I share my dream with won't support it, and may even oppose it. But that's okay if wise, godly, prayerful people support my dream. They confirm it's God's voice and not my ego that's speaking. There is objective confirmation, not just subjective.

6. The Test of Decision

Where am I in the decision on my dream? For it to be from God, it surely needs to be 'who decides' not 'what is decided'. I need to ask myself which of these following three positions am I taking:

a) am I wanting to simply make a decision before God, without any real intention to get around to doing it?

b) am I bargaining with God, ensuring I get at least a little of what I want while feeling I've 'taken the matter' to Him?

c) or am I seeking God's will alone?

It is, of course, the last of these that reveals my dream truly is God's dream for me. The words that opened this chapter come from the prophet Joel and were quoted by Saint Peter in his speech to the crowd at Pentecost. That humble fisherman, who brought thousands to the Lord, was a source of inspiration for me throughout this mission. Despite often making mistakes, he was humble enough to know that he needed to listen to the Lord. Is the Lord asking you to step out of the boat like he did Peter? Is he asking you to make that dream of yours a reality? The time to answer that question is now.

*Millie, Jasmine and Paul
at Weymouth.*

*BBC Radio Solent's coverage
of our homecoming*

*Arriving home at Hamble to family, friends
and Celebrate Southampton*

APPENDIX

FURTHER CREW TESTIMONIES

ANN KERR - ARBROATH TO INVERNESS

We had the time of our lives sailing with the Celebrate Sailing Mission on one of the Scottish legs, from Arbroath to Inverness. It was a spectacular journey in the hands of one of the most skilled yachtsmen we have met. Russ was the perfect host and friend. We made friends with some wonderful people that I know will impact our lives and our faith journey in the months and years to follow. We exchanged stories of our lives, laughed, cried, prayed, sang and even had a wee dance together. We will remember this experience for the rest of our lives. God Bless Celebrate and Joel's Bar. Proud to have been a part of it all.

FRAN GRAHAM - SWANSEA TO CARDIFF

As soon as I heard about the Sailing Mission, I felt excitement which I believe was from God. I am so glad I did it. I can't remember a time that I felt so carefree or laughed so much as I did onboard. I felt God's love almost tangibly onboard! Because we all accepted each other and laughed and had fun, it was full of joy! We were doing it for God but I felt that He was carrying us along and looking after us. Even when once or twice the sea got a bit choppy, I felt safe. This all increased my faith.

There were many highlights: doing a prayer walk in Swansea centre before setting out the next day; praying on the open sea with Russ and Ingrid; being with lovely Christians and being part of the crew and learning the ropes, literally! Also - sharing our lives and having meals together. I feel that this is true community and belonging to Jesus, and this was how the Apostles felt being with Jesus. We had a little party onboard after the gathering on the quayside in Cardiff, and it was so lovely when all the people came onboard.

MARIA MCCARTHY - PLYMOUTH TO DARTMOUTH

Being part of a united nationwide prayer surrounding our country was the primary reason that we wanted to be involved in the mission. It was an opportunity to be part of a wonderful adventure for the glory of our Lord. Holding a praise and worship meeting on the quayside of the Barbican, Plymouth had profound spiritual significance. This was where the pilgrim fathers set off in faith to a new world. Here we were in 2019, being witnesses to the joy and hope of Christ in our world today. It was a beautiful experience of praying in the spirit and being instruments of healing and evangelisation. We were blessed to have Fr Jon and Fr Oscar praying with passers-by during our worship.

Alan and I were privileged to sail out of Plymouth Sound and along the beautiful South Devon coast to Dartmouth. The atmosphere on the boat was filled with the Holy Spirit, and as we sailed, chatted, ate and prayed, there was an atmosphere of peace and joy and hope. I knew that the Holy Spirit was encircling our land, protecting and cherishing it. How little did we know a year ago, that not only our country, but the whole world would be in need of prayer due to the Coronavirus.

During lockdown, my spirit continually returned to that experience of being on the water and praying for our country. It was looking at a familiar coastline from the very different perspective of the sea that had a profound effect on me. It was as if the Lord was showing me how he sees the bigger picture. He can see within and without, right and left and yet I am limited to just one perspective. Furthermore, I was still having physical difficulties with my own vision. He was asking me to trust and surrender on the sea of life but was challenging me to embrace a wider vision. A vision that incorporates peace, hope and joy that can only be accomplished through total reliance on him. I had a clear choice - stay limited in safety or sail out in faith.

ANGELA SLATTERY - LYMINGTON TO HAMBLE

I heard about the mission from Russ at one of our Southampton Celebrate core team meetings. The date was still about a year away and as I was still working full-time, I didn't even think that I might be able to take part onboard but put the date of the Hamble quayside send off in my diary, determined to feel part of the mission.

After the (delayed) send-off I enthusiastically followed the Facebook updates as the various crews made their way round the coast. Whilst round at my daughter and son-in-law David's house, Dave said that as he had been unable to be part of the sail-off crew due to the delayed start, he was going to do the final leg instead. For a variety of reasons, I (or maybe the Lord) had decided to retire two months earlier than originally intended and had booked a week away to unwind. I was getting home on two days before Dave was heading off! When I first processed the dates in my head, my heart sank. Russ was already on the trip; I couldn't join now – could I? Then Dave said, 'I'm organising the crew for that final leg, if you want to join, just say'.

We were blessed with amazing weather for the last leg. I hadn't sailed for over 40 years but through Russ' teaching I soon felt like part of the crew. Having had such a busy couple of years before retiring I loved the peace of being away from the clutter of my life, the enormity of the sea and sky and little old me in the great expanse. It has helped me declutter my life since returning.

The experience helped me with my prayer life which had become very dry. Sailing past the Fawley refinery port was special for me as I help with the Apostleship of the Sea mission work there. I also felt a spiritual/family bond with the others who had been part of the mission. Russ, Dave and I shared many stories whilst sailing and I feel it has helped to unite us more in our continued work on the Southampton Celebrate core team.

Arriving back at Hamble quayside was amazing. Such love and giving praise to God was a truly wonderful thing to witness. The whole experience will stay with me forever. If given the opportunity I would definitely do it again.

*For more testimonies, photos of the mission
and details of what Russ is up to now,
visit the Celebrate Sailing facebook page:
facebook.com/CelebrateSailing*

ACKNOWLEDGEMENTS

I would like to thank God for planting this dream on my heart, the Holy Spirit for helping us every step of the way, and my dear wife Deirdre for supporting me on this mission. Her blessing my absence from home for three months, and her assurance when I had doubts about the sanity of coming out of work, were instrumental to the success of the whole endeavour.

So many people have helped make this dream become a reality: the prayer warriors who signed up as crew; Jenny Baker and the Celebrate leadership team for endorsing the watery pilgrimage; the evangelists who turned out on the quayside to praise the Lord and engage with people. They were all inspirational, as were the many people who held us in prayer to keep us safe and lead people to the Lord through our witness on the quaysides.

None more so than Sue Whitehead and her husband Charles, who spurred me on with so much love and encouragement, not to mention little gifts of comfort, given to me at several quayside gatherings en route - thank you.

A very big 'thank you' to my dear friend John McKenna, for interviewing me and the many crew, and putting this amazing story into words for this book, which I would have gotten around to some-time never. Praying that his faithfulness and writing skills will help others to be inspired to follow their own God-given dreams.

*Further copies of this book
can be obtained from*

Goodnews Books
*Upper level
St. John's Church Complex
296 Sundon Park Road
Luton, Beds. LU3 3AL*

*www.goodnewsbooks.net
orders@goodnewsbooks.net
01582 571011*

and from Amazon.co.uk